Mindful Motivation

Combine Mindfulness and Drive to Create a
Life of Meaning, Purpose and Peace

Collected Writings

Gudjon Bergmann

ISBN: 978-1-7372093-1-7
Publisher: Flaming Leaf Press
Copyright 2023 Gudjon Bergmann.
All rights reserved.

Table of Contents

Introduction - 1
Section 1) Mindful Moments - 9
Section 2) Motivation - 79
Section 3) Models - 143
Section 4) Seeking Help - 189
About the Author - 203

Foreword: Broad Collection

This book includes a broad collection of ideas and practices I've been gathering and creating since the 90s. The writings come from articles, books, and unpublished drafts. Each chapter describes an idea or practice, so you don't need to read the book from front to back. Feel free to jump around and explore what interests you.

Gudjon Bergmann

Be Here, Get There

Be at peace. Strive for goals. Go to a monastery for one, business school for the other. The two approaches have historically been at odds with each other.

Increasingly, though, people are waking up and realizing that they want both. They want to be more mindful and present while pursuing where they want to go.

I am one of those people.

Primary Influences

I got introduced to the teachings of the monk and poet Thich Nhat Hanh and motivational speaker and author Brian Tracy around the same time. I was in my twenties, had made a mess, and was in the process of turning my life around. I still have beaten-up copies of Hanh's *Being Peace* (1987) and Tracy's *Maximum Achievement* (1993). During my transition from party-dude to service-oriented helper, I sought council from them near-daily.

The Teachings of Thich Nhat Hanh

Since then, I've read much of what Thich Nhat Hanh wrote and published during his long and influential life. Yet, the teachings that stayed with me came from my initial introduction to mindful living. Here are several quotes from *Being Peace* that still resonate deeply.

"Breathing in, I calm body and mind. Breathing out, I smile. Dwelling in the present moment, I know this is the only moment."

"In modern society, most of us don't want to be in touch with ourselves; we want to be in touch with other things like religion, sports, politics, a book—we want to forget ourselves. Anytime we have leisure, we want to invite something else to enter us, opening ourselves to the television and telling the television to come and colonize us."

"If in our daily life, we can smile, if we can be peaceful and happy, not only we, but everyone, will profit from it. This is the most basic kind of peace work."

"I would not look upon anger as something foreign to me that I have to fight... I have to deal with my anger with care, with love, with tenderness, with nonviolence."

"The problem is whether we are determined to go in the direction of compassion or not. If we are, then can we reduce the suffering to a minimum? If I lose my direction, I have to look for the North Star, and I go to the north. That does not mean I expect to arrive at the North Star. I just want to go in that direction."

His teachings about staying present, being aware of distractions, spreading peace, and dealing with difficult emotions were all eye-opening. And his *"never arriving at the North Star even though traveling in that direction"* metaphor illustrated that he advocated against the idea of perfection. He remained humble and introspective throughout his life.

The Teachings of Brian Tracy

After attending the Pheonix seminar in 1996, I bought a copy of the audio program *Accelerated Learning Techniques* by Tracy and listened to it countless times. From that time until 2007 or 2008, I never listened to the radio, which Tracy aptly dubbed as *"chewing gum for the ears,"* but instead listened to audio programs. Tracy supplied a substantial part of my audio library, covering everything from self-worth and selling techniques to forgiveness, time management and success. Here are some of his ideas that still drive me today.

"You cannot control what happens to you, but you can control your attitude toward what happens to you, and in that, you will be mastering change rather than allowing it to master you."

"All successful people are big dreamers. They imagine what their future could be, ideal in every respect, and then they work every day toward their distant vision, goal or purpose."

"The ability to discipline yourself to delay gratification in the short term in order to enjoy greater rewards in the long term is the indispensable prerequisite for success."

"Your life only gets better when you get better."

"A goal without a plan is only a dream."

"There is never enough time to do everything, but there is always enough time to do the most important thing."

Because I want to be compassionate, Tracy's focus on creating win-win situations rather than dominating others kept me coming back to his teachings. I also found empowerment in the idea of self-reliance and often chanted his favorite phrase, *"if it's to be, it's up to me."*

Adopting the Right Attitude

Naturally, the teachings of these two men appear to be at odds. Thich Nhat Hanh told me that the present moment is the only moment. Brian Tracy urged me to focus on the future, work hard, manage my time, and improve myself. It took me a few years to figure out the right balance, but I finally realized that the two approaches supplement each other—if I adopt the right attitude.

The reward is a life where both teachings support my values. Mindfulness helps me to be here and create moments of peace. Clear goals give my life purpose and meaning. I don't have to choose between them. Neither do you.

Variations on These Themes

The following chapters are variations on these two themes. Some focus more on goal setting and self-improvement, others on mindfulness and balance. Because this is a collection of published and unpublished writings, there is some repetition. Still, reading all the chapters will give you a balanced view of both and offer ways to implement them in your daily life.

Mindful Moments

"The flesh endures the storms of the present alone, the mind those of the past and future as well."

Epicurus

The Mindfulness Cycle

The practice of being mindful has four parts —five if you count the hidden one (which we will). First, you focus on a subject or object of your choosing. Second, your mind wanders. This is both normal and natural. Third, you notice that your mind has wandered. Fourth, you bring your attention back to the subject or object of your choosing. That's it.

What to Focus On?

The subject or object of focus usually comes from one of three categories: external, physical, or mental. Externally, you can focus on a candle, nature sounds, pictures, music, or even send love and light to other people through what has been called loving-kindness meditation. Physically, you can focus on breathing, movement or physical sensations. Mentally, you can focus on words and images or learn to be aware of your thoughts.

Allowing the Mind to Wander

I've taught meditation since 1997 and have found that one of the biggest obstacles most people face is unhappiness when their mind starts to wander. "My mind is not doing what I want it to do. I can't keep my focus," they cry in desperation. Explaining that wandering is the nature of the mind often takes more than one try. But when people get it, they learn to work with the mind instead of against its nature.

Noticing

People can get so involved in thoughts that they don't notice when their mind has wandered until several minutes have passed. Noticing is an observation skill that requires a certain detachment from thoughts. You need to see them from afar. Learning to step back and notice thoughts instead of getting caught in them is a skill just like focusing, which means that it can be learned.

Returning to Focus

In his classic, *A Path With Heart*, Jack Kornfield likens training the mind to training a puppy. Instead of getting angry whenever the puppy does something wrong, an intelligent dog owner learns to use positive reinforcement and keeps bringing the puppy back to the preferred behavior.

In the same way, it is easy to get frustrated with yourself when you are practicing mindfulness. Be smart and gently bring your mind to your chosen point of focus.

Circular Practice

Whether you are focusing on walking, a sunset, your child, a prayer, your breath or something else, the practice is always the same. You concentrate, your mind wanders, you notice it has wandered, and then you return to your point of focus. Over time, you will get better at focusing for longer periods, but the mind will always wander, whether for short or prolonged periods. Accepting this is key to practicing mindfulness.

The Fifth Part: Being

The fifth part of mindfulness is not something you consciously do. It is a state of being that sometimes occurs between focusing and wandering. For instance, when you get fully immersed in any repetitive focus, from meditation to long-distance running, there is often a space of being that opens between focus and wandering. Your mind feels empty and full simultaneously, yet you are not really focusing on anything, and your mind has not yet begun to wander. You simply are.

Some people are in such a hurry to master the practice of focusing that they mistake being for wandering and bring their mind back to the point of focus. Instead, I encourage you to enjoy each moment of being when it occurs. You can't manufacture being on demand, but you can savor it when it presents itself. The mind will wander soon enough. Then you can return to the circular practice, during which you may encounter being again.

How to Get Started

If you follow these guidelines, getting started is relatively easy. Choose what you want to focus on—external, physical or mental—and commit to the process. Approach mindfulness as a stand-alone practice or bring awareness into everything you do. The choice is yours.

Principles of Mindfulness

Life can sometimes feel like an unrelenting storm, probably more often than we'd like to admit. The average person faces problems all the time and enters crisis mode on a regular basis. Some people numb themselves to this reality, whereas others seek constructive solutions.

Embracing Impermanency

Being inherently restless, peace has not come easily to me. Growing up, I experienced family trauma and bullying that caused me to abuse alcohol in my teens and twenties. When I finally quit drinking and turned my life around in 1999, I began pursuing happiness, success, and inner peace through all possible means. I became a yoga and meditation teacher, created a booming speaking business, wrote books, and kept adding to my entrepreneurial and emotional skills. I flourished. Well into my thirties, I was sure that my trajectory would never stop.

My forties brought me back to earth and taught me humility. I had to navigate difficult times, sometimes hardly managing to keep my head above water. To stay sober and sane, I was forced to change. Instead of aiming for permanent peace and never-ending-improvement, I learned to embrace occasional moments of peace with more serenity and be okay with it when I had to re-enter the storm of life, however much it battered me.

As you will see on subsequent pages, this new way of thinking completely changed my approach to meditation and relaxation. I replaced expectations of enlightenment with a stoic appreciation of impermanency.

Three Guiding Principles

Principles are defined as fundamental to our beliefs, behaviors, and reasoning. Clear principles are shortcuts that allow us to move through life with relative ease. Fuzzy principles can cause tremendous inner stress and grind decision-making to a halt. This means that if we are to create moments of peace in life, we need principles that support our efforts, especially when life is hectic.

As the brief overview of my story illustrated, relief from stress became harder to find in my forties, so I had to re-examine the principles that had guided me for almost two decades. I stumbled around in the dark for a while until I landed on three philosophically consistent principles that replaced the old ones.

When I started showing my new principles to others, I realized I was onto something universal. Typical reactions were, "of course," "this makes total sense," and "hey, I have been talking about this 'moments of peace thing' with my wife, and it has been really helpful." It wasn't just me. Others were also stuck in a flawed paradigm, waiting for life to become more peaceful instead of appreciating moments of peace here and now.

Here are the three guiding principles I uncovered. See if they make as much sense to you as they did to me.

Principle 1) Impermanency

Time passes. All moments are impermanent. Plainly speaking, this means that peace is not a destination. Instead, moments of peace are like rest stops on the highway of life. They can be short (fleeting) or long (moments in time), but they are always temporary. This idea is not new. The philosophy of impermanency has risen to the surface in various traditions over the millennia. It reminds us that change is the only constant. All anyone has is the present moment.

Principle 2) Peace is Relative

The concept of relativity can be summed up with the words: It depends. Even though most people have a sense of what is peaceful, feelings of peace depend on circumstances.

For example, imagine being in a construction zone. A jackhammer is going full force. The sound is deafening. Suddenly, the jackhammer stops. Ahh. What relief. Even though there is plenty of noise in the background, it feels peaceful when the eardrum-trashing stops.

Now, imagine being at home trying to meditate in silence. The sink starts dripping. The sound, which you would not have heard in the construction zone, is disproportionately loud. Your moment of peace is disturbed.

As these examples show, feelings of peace depend on various things, such as activity, mental and emotional states, surroundings, degrees of disruption, and more. Equipped with that understanding, we should never accept other people's definitions of peace without first comparing their lives to our own. Looking at how a monk practices peace in seclusion may not fit the mold of a teacher with three children whose moment of peace can be a cup of coffee before the kids wake up.

I've made this mistake several times over the years, looking at other people without comparing their situations and life stories with mine. Acknowledging relativity allows us to experience moments of peace relative to our circumstances.

Principle 3) Practice is the Goal

Because moments are impermanent, no one can deposit moments of peace into a bank account and then become permanently peaceful in the future. Peace does not accumulate. Instead, peaceful practices are in the same category as brushing teeth—a twice-daily activity with no clear final objective vital to dental health.

This is important. Many people feel they should be better than they are just because they've practiced meditation for years. That's like brushing your teeth with the expectation of achieving perfect dental health at some point in the future. Not realistic.

It can be freeing to let go of the myth of a peaceful destination and shift the commitment to a chosen activity instead, such as breathing, walking, meditating, relaxing, taking a bath, or any other form of mental and emotional hygiene.

The practice then becomes the goal. Nothing more, nothing less. It's doing for the sake of doing.

Integrating the Principles

Honestly, it took me a few months to fully integrate these principles into my life. I had to let go of old beliefs and thought patterns while reminding myself of the evident nature of the new principles.

It was especially difficult to let go of the idea of 'permanent enlightenment' and replace it with 'peace sometimes.' I kept reminding myself that life would never be stress-free, which is okay.

The second principle spurred me to embrace peace in many forms, anything from a deep breath at the traffic lights to playing cards with the family. I am still finding subtle ways to enjoy moments relative to my circumstances. For me, the easiest principle to integrate was probably the third one. I was quickly able to change my mindset and approach my mindfulness practices with a sense of non-attachment. Each practice session became its reward.

Now that you've heard my story, it's your turn. Consider the implications on your own life as you answer the following questions.

Impermanency: What would life look like if you stopped waiting for it to become more peaceful (destination) and instead savored each moment of peace, willing to let go when it was over?

Relativity: What would it feel like if—instead of wishing that life was as peaceful as it was back in the day or chasing someone else's definition of peace that is far removed from your current circumstances—you could enjoy moments of peace that are relative to your life as it is today?

Goal: What if, while practicing, you could silence the voice that keeps saying, "are we there yet," and focus instead on the practice without any expectations?

Seven Metaphors

I've spent thousands of hours as a non-academic teacher and facilitator since the late nineties. Because I never teach to a test, I am always on the lookout for what sticks and why? What do people comment on when I meet them after a successful seminar? What do they mention in emails and comments?

Three things have stuck out.

First, people remember stories. The more personal and preferably embarrassing, the better, but any story will do, even ones about other people.

Second, people remember step-by-step instructions. I've been stopped on the street numerous times by people thanking me for detailed relaxation and meditation instructions that helped them change their lives.

Third, people remember metaphors. Unlike facts, metaphors honor everything that a person already knows. Connecting something known to something unknown allows them to tap into their fountain of knowledge and experience. I cannot count the number of times someone in my seminars responded to a metaphor by saying, "You mean that..." and added tremendous insights I'd never thought of before.

The Multiplication Effect

When I was first asked to give a presentation about creating moments of mindfulness, I had those three to choose from. I decided to focus first and foremost on metaphors because I wanted to honor what people already knew.

Overview:

The Anchor is about being present.
The Bandwidth refers to the conscious mind.
The Steering Wheel addresses control or lack thereof.
The Instinct is a reminder to listen.
The Weather is an age-old metaphor for emotions.
The Current revolves around energy states.
The Tower offers a meditation approach based on an ancient story.

Some will resonate with you more than others. Listen to that. If one or two metaphors help you add moments of mindfulness, reading this book was time well spent. The more you contemplate each metaphor, the more you'll own the outcome. Your additions are the secret ingredient.

Metaphor 1. The Anchor

The mind can be in more than two places at once. In fact, the mind can be all over the place. I know mine can. The body, however, can only be here and now. It is immovable from the present moment. That is why the body is the ideal anchor for the mind. Anytime the mind is restless, stuck in the past, or worried about the future, drop the anchor by focusing intently on the body.

I ran a yoga studio for five years and saw the benefits of anchoring daily. It was amazing to see how people shed stress with every deep breath, every stretch, and each reminder to be in the moment.

In addition to traditional Eastern practices, a variety of modern mindfulness techniques rely on this approach. People are encouraged to anchor using methods such as exploring a raisin with the tongue, bringing awareness to physical exercises—everything from weightlifting to walking—and focusing on the beating heart.

Most everyone agrees that the breath is the quickest way to anchor the mind to the body. Heed the universal advice of taking a few deep breaths during times of distress.

Whichever method you choose, anchoring is an ancient technique that works. Intensity can vary based on circumstances. Breathing can be vigorous or subtle, movements minimal or powerful. The choice is yours. Just remember that if the mind is all over the place, do what it takes to anchor it to the body.

Anchor Summary:

- The body is an anchor for the mind.
- Conscious breathing quickly connects the mind to the body.

Metaphor 2. The Bandwidth

If you've ever cried out, "the internet is too slow," you instinctively understand the concept of limited bandwidth. Internet bandwidth determines the amount of data that devices can access. A crowded bandwidth leads to a slower data flow. Less congestion in the bandwidth leads to more speed. To mix metaphors, it's the difference between rush hour traffic in New York and an eight-lane superhighway with only a few cars on it.

The mind's bandwidth is similar, limited by what we can be consciously aware of. We all know from experience that a thousand competing thoughts coming from all sides will lead to anxiety and irritation, whereas a few thoughts floating around in our awareness will make us feel calmer. This metaphor underlines that. The more crowded the bandwidth, the less peace, and the less crowded the more peace.

Contrary to popular belief, however, the bandwidth cannot be emptied entirely. There is always something going on, no matter how subtle, such as bodily functions, ambient sounds, and occasional thoughts.

To create moments of mindfulness, the goal is simply to reduce the number of items in the bandwidth. This is done by addressing three sources: External input, internal output, and concentration.

This metaphor is more complex than the others and may seem a little convoluted. Please take a moment to wrap your mind around it. For me, guarding the bandwidth has become an essential part of life.

External Input: Be Like a Turtle

The first step is to reduce external input. The primary senses are sight and sound, so most people start by reducing noise or replacing it with white noise or music (hearing) and closing their eyes (sight). Addressing the primary senses may be enough for some, but I've also found it important to consider the other senses. Harsh smells, bad tastes, and extreme heat or cold can be irritants. To create a moment of mindfulness, be like a turtle and withdraw the five senses into your shell as well as you can.

Internal Output: Letting Go

Once the external input has been reduced or simplified, it is natural for subconscious thoughts—such as dreams, worries, fears, etc.—to stream into the bandwidth. What comes up can be a mixed bag.

In all honesty, addressing the internal output is likely the most challenging aspect of this metaphor because it's not like we can turn it off. However, it's good to know that nearly all meditation traditions urge people to deal with the subconscious mind in the same way, with the practice of non-attachment. This means letting go of thoughts as they arise instead of holding onto them; witnessing thoughts instead of being an active thinker; taking a step back, and watching mental traffic from afar. I especially like that last one. Being stuck in thoughts can be like traffic, loud and messy, whereas non-attachment is like sitting at the top of a grassy hill, seeing the traffic from afar, and only hearing faint sounds from time to time. The practice of non-attachment doesn't remove thoughts but usually creates distance so we don't get caught up in them.

If thoughts persist and the practice of non-attachment is not working, getting help from a seasoned mental health practitioner can help. I know from experience that most meditation retreats would benefit significantly from the presence of such professionals.

Concentration: Fewer Thoughts

Concentration is the act of partially filling the bandwidth with a mental construct of your choice. The focus is usually on a single word, phrase, or image. This technique is the foundation for most meditation practices. Those who don't want to meditate, however, can achieve similar calming effects by focusing on a simple repetitive task, such as walking, running, woodwork, sowing, or playing an instrument, to name a few. This is known as '*the zone*' or '*flow*' and has been well-documented. No matter the approach, replacing many thoughts with a single thought, an image, a visualization, or an activity has been shown to lead to moments of mindfulness.

Less Congestion Equals More Peace

Overall, your choice of practices to reduce activity in the bandwidth needs to be flexible. For instance, you may create a profound moment of mindfulness through breathing and relaxation one day but be so overwhelmed with work (external input) and worries (internal output) another day that listening to classical music while puzzling is a better recipe. No matter the approach, the formula remains simple. Less congestion equals more peace.

Bandwidth Summary:

- More crowded = Less peace
- Less crowded = More peace

Metaphor 3. The Steering Wheel

Imagine being in traffic, obsessed with what everyone else is doing, wishing you could control their cars, yet having no power to change their behavior. It would drive you nuts.

The steering wheel is a metaphor for what we can control. Ancient Stoics, Greek and Roman, took this idea to heart when they proclaimed that followers should only focus on what they could control and be indifferent to everything else.

They were onto something.

People generally feel powerless and miserable when they focus on things out of their control. The more you focus on others, the worse you'll feel, but the more you focus on what you can control, the better you'll feel and the easier it will be to create moments of mindfulness.

Steering Wheel Summary:

- Understand what you can't control.
- Focus on controlling what you can.

Metaphor 4. The Instinct

The instinct is less of a metaphor and more of a reminder to listen. Human beings are animals that have instincts. We forget this at our peril. Two instincts deserve special attention.

One is the *"fight or flight"* response. It occurs when real (or imagined) danger sets off a chemical reaction that causes a person to want to fight or flee. It can be helpful when that person can jump into action but harmful when all it does is fuel emotions, causing people to spin out of control.

Learning to deal with this response is a lifelong process. I've found it helpful to think of *"fight or flight"* as a surge of energy. Imagine that you've come to a fork in the road every time it happens. One avenue leads to action; the other fuels an emotional spiral that stays on the inside. If action is available, take that avenue. The energy will help you act, then dissolve. If action is unavailable, do what you can to calm down or attempt to get rid of the excess energy through some form of exercise.

The polar opposite is the instinct to rest and recover. Looking at the animal kingdom, all animals rest naturally when needed. However, because human beings have a faculty that allows them to override instincts—most beneficial for survival—they have learned how to override the instinct for rest in a 24/7 society that makes endless demands and offers easy access to distractions.

The result is that too many people are not getting enough rest. This lack of recovery time leads to a slew of problems, physical, mental, and emotional issues. To turn this trend around, start listening to the body's instinct to rest and only override it when necessary... not just to watch another episode of your favorite series.

Listening to the body and responding accordingly, especially when the instinct is to rest, is a vital part of the quest to create moments of mindfulness.

Instinct Summary:

- Listen to the instinct to rest and recover.
- Use the *"fight or flight"* response only when appropriate.
- Dissipate stress energy when harmful or unnecessary.

Metaphor 5. The Weather

Don't like the weather?
Just wait a minute.

It's a joke that has become popular in many parts of the world, and it points to an important truth. The weather is constantly changing.

Comparing emotions to ever-changing weather cements the concept of impermanency. In the same way that those atmospheric systems don't stay in the same place forever, no feeling is final. Distress will pass. Moments of peace will also pass.

The big difference between weather systems and emotions is that you have some control over your emotional states. You may not be able to control every emotion, but you can influence them with your thoughts and responses. Mental tools such as mindfulness, positive thinking, affirmations, cognitive behavioral therapy, etc., can help.

Just remember that influence is not the same as total control.

Because emotions fluctuate, we must note how we talk about them. Two psychiatrists, who attended one of my seminars several years ago, told me that disease labels were there to diagnose, not to be used as additions to people's personalities. The implication was that once an emotion is noted in the personal possessive (my), it becomes harder to see its changing nature. This means that addressing emotions in the third person can help create some distance, as in "a sadness" instead of "my sadness."

Mental awareness is key. I come from Iceland, where four seasons can show up within four hours. A certain degree of resiliency and flexibility comes from dealing with such external volatility. Thankfully, most people don't have an emotional constitution that resembles the Icelandic climate. Nevertheless, it's natural for emotional states to change. Be prepared to hunker down for storms and enjoy the sun when it shines. Most importantly, remember the ancient Persian saying, *"this too shall pass."*

Weather Summary:

- Treat emotions like the weather (constantly changing).
- Influence internal conditions by creating moments of mindfulness.
- Be okay with letting go of the calm, knowing it will return.

Metaphor 6. The Current

The current is the animating force that makes human beings go. Like electricity, it is invisible to the naked eye. Yet, people are aware of it daily, and it occupies language easily. We talk about it when we have "a lot of energy" or "not very much energy" and quickly assess whether or not other people are energetic.

The current can be split into three categories that resemble states of water.

- Swamp = Lethargy, sadness, exhaustion, and decline.
- River = Intensity, passion, irritability, and stress.

- Lake = Calm, peace, power, and depth.

Swamp energy is stagnant. River energy is intense. Lake energy is calm. All three have their purpose in life, but if you want to create moments of mindfulness, nurture the calm energy.

The cyclical nature of these three energy states is intriguing. The current naturally moves from lethargy (swamp) to intensity (river) to calm (lake), then back to lethargy, and so on. The cycle is neverending. Flowing water clears up the stagnant swamp. A calm deep vessel pools the flowing water, becoming a lake. Turn off the flow, and the lake becomes a swamp again.

This energy loop influences the quest for moments of mindfulness directly. Let's say that you decide to wake up early and meditate but are tired and can hardly keep your eyes open. With the cyclical nature of energy in mind, you need to increase your energy with movement or breathing before calming down for meditation. Going straight from being sleepy to being calm will result in more sleepiness. The path from lazy to calm always moves through some intensity.

This metaphor underlines two things. One, that energy is needed to eliminate laziness before entering a calm state. Two, staying too long in a calm state can become laziness. No one can prevent the current from circulating naturally. Still, we can choose to rise out of lethargy with energy and then take breaks when the energy becomes erratic, intense, or stressful by creating moments of mindfulness.

Current Summary:

- Understand the cyclical nature of the current.
- Utilize calm energy to create moments of peace.

Metaphor 7. The Tower

The final metaphor comes in the form of an ancient story.

One day, a master called a favorite student and said: "You have done so well that I have decided to give you one of my treasured possessions."

The student thought for a moment, then asked: "I can choose anything?"

"Yes, anything."

"Then I would like the wish-granting genie," the student said.

"Are you sure?" the master replied. "The genie will grant your wishes, but you must keep it busy at all times; otherwise, it will destroy you."

The student answered with complete confidence: "Yes, I am sure. I have so many wishes. I doubt that the genie will ever be able to grant them all."

And so, the student got the wish-granting-genie.

Two weeks later, a visibly anxious, unkempt, and exhausted student returned to the master, exclaiming: "Master, master! You must help me. It started out great. I wished for things I thought would take the genie days to complete, only to find them done in a matter of hours. Within a week, I had run out of wishes. I have been running and hiding ever since, hoping the genie would not find me and destroy me. What should I do? What should I do???"

The master answered in a calm voice: "The genie is powerful and difficult to control. You did the right thing by coming here. What you do now is call the genie and tell it to build a sky-high tower. Then you say, 'Genie, go up and down the tower until I call you.' That way, the genie will always have something to do, and you won't have to worry."

The Moral of the Story

The genie represents the rational mind. It can produce great achievements when focused and cause distress when distracted or untethered. Based on that understanding, we should all do as the student did and create our own towers.

An internal tower can keep the mind occupied when it is not engaged.

Traditionally, an inner tower is a word, phrase, image, or prayer. The great thing about this approach is that once an internal tower has been built, it can be used both while pausing between tasks and during meditation. The tower becomes the go-to resting place for the mind when it is not busy with something productive.

Tower Summary:

- Choose a word, phrase, image, or prayer for your tower.
- Send the mind to the tower when not occupied.
- If you meditate, use the same word, phrase, image, or prayer during practice.

Information is Not Free

We live in an era of unmatched access to information. Anything you want to learn is at your fingertips. Necessary or unnecessary, who cares? Let's learn everything. It's free, after all.

Not so fast.

The intake of information is indeed free. Processing is another matter. In computer terms, every data entered into the brain must be processed, labeled as necessary or needless, and filed away or deleted.

The larger the intake, the more energy and time it takes to process the information. What seemed free is now expensive.

No Room for Mindfulness

This is one of the biggest hurdles I face with clients. They are constantly taking in information but never allow for processing time. Therefore, when they try to make room for mindfulness, the mind is flooded with thoughts and images, which is the mind's attempt to process the data that has been consumed.

Two Possible Solutions

This problem has two possible solutions.

One, reduce the intake of information. That is harder than it sounds. Unless you want to keep the TV turned off, focus only on work during computer time, and only touch your phone if it rings, you will be exposed to much more information than your contemporaries twenty or thirty years ago. That's just the way life is now. Still, with some effort, it is possible to filter the information and reduce the number of exposures throughout the day.

Two, make time for processing. The subconscious mind needs time to filter and sort, in addition to all the other stuff it does when we are unaware. Taking quiet walks, baths, or engaging in simple forms of repetitive activities, such as gardening and crafts, will allow the mind to process.

If You Don't Make Time to Process

If you don't make time for processing, the best-case scenario is that it will happen during your attempts at mindfulness or meditation, and peace will elude you.

In the worst-case scenario, processing will intrude on your sleep. I've seen many cases where insomnia is caused because the mind cannot slow down. And even when they know the culprit, people's addiction to constant information intake still wins. Their phones are on from the time they wake up until the moment they attempt to go to sleep. At that point, it's like taking the lid off an overflowing trash can.

Be Mindful of Your Intake

I've never been one of those who rail against modern man's advances. Having information at my fingertips is valuable. I don't want to turn back the clock. However, with every advancement, we discover new problems that need to be solved. Overstimulation of the brain is one such problem. As we seek solutions, we can, at least, be mindful and remember that the intake of information has a hidden cost; processing.

Mindful Intention Goals

Most goals are focused on specific outcomes. Lose 10 pounds, increase salary or savings, create a product, get a new job, and so on. Each can be measured. You either lose the weight and get the job... or you don't.

Mindful intention goals are different. They focus on bringing specific values into circumstances and acting in accordance with those values. The focus is on the process rather than the outcome—intention and input.

For instance, someone can say: "To be more mindful (value) with my partner tonight (situation), I will turn off the phone, listen intently and be fully present (actions)."

Begin With Values

Lately, I've been working with several clients on mindful intention goals. The process starts with uncovering their most important values. When approached correctly, intention goals allow you to live with more fulfillment as you bring those values into everyday situations.

There are several ways to uncover values. You can dream about the future, look at what is most important to you, and look at the needs you want to fulfill. The values can include anything from mindfulness to adventure. Consider the following list for inspiration:

- Mindfulness
- Awareness
- Honesty
- Adventure
- Excitement
- Peace
- Presence
- Love
- Compassion
- Industry

Use This Stem Sentence

Once you have a personalized list of the values you want to include more often in your life, use the following stem to set your intention goals. A stem is a fill-in-the-blank sentence that you can use for various situations.

"To [enter value] in [enter situation],
I will [enter actions]."

Stem Samples

- To be more compassionate (value) in this meeting today (situation), I will prepare my points, take a deep breath every time I am tempted to interject with force, and make my case factually (actions).

- To honor my need for aloneness (value) today (situation), I will take a walk around the neighborhood and listen to my thoughts and feelings (actions).

- To be more passionate (value) on this trip with my significant other (situation), I will bring energy, nurture feelings of love, be spontaneous, listen to my partner's needs and wants, and approach everything we do with awe and excitement (actions).

- To be more peaceful (value) as I protest this injustice (situation), I will nurture feelings of peace, raise my voice with honor, and resist the actions rather than allow myself to hate the doer (actions).

Variety of Situations

You can use the stem sentence to create mindful intention goals throughout the day; when you wake, eat breakfast, at work, with your family, and in all extracurricular activities. The overarching goal is to bring more *mindfulness* and *intention* to everything in life.

Practice, Practice, Practice

Two of my clients come to mind. One wrote a long list of values, learned the stem sentence, then told me in earnest one month later that he had not practiced at all— something he plans to remedy. Another wrote two primary values and practiced making intentional goals with them every day and in all situations for over a month. She felt significant improvements in her life as a result.

The key is practice. Intention goals are the same as brushing your teeth, making the bed, eating and meditating. Repetition is needed for them to become habitual.

Meditation Building Blocks

Consider the following. When you learned how to read, you first learned the letters, then how to combine them into words, then to form sentences with words, paragraphs with sentences, and you became better with practice.

Learning meditation is much the same.

There is learning. There is practice. There is more learning. More practice. And you keep on going until you achieve the meditative state.

There are no shortcuts.

Unlike the letters in the alphabet, the building blocks of meditation are understanding, relaxation and concentration.

- If you don't understand, you won't practice.
- If you cannot relax, meditation becomes difficult.

- If you cannot concentrate, meditation is nearly impossible.

What is Meditation?

The terms relaxation, concentration and meditation are not synonymous. The following definitions can help you remove confusion.

Relaxation: A state between waking and sleeping, where the body is completely still, and the mind is allowed to flow freely from one thought to another, or alternately, become unwittingly calm. It is a rejuvenating and energizing state. Where laziness drains energy, relaxation provides energy. You don't have to empty the mind. Simply calm the body.

Concentration: A mental state where the stream of consciousness flows in a single direction, or alternately, a state in which the mind is alert and aware. For meditation, concentration should be relaxed.

Meditation: A state best described as *dreamless sleep while awake*. Mental activity is reduced to a point where the mind feels empty but is not; the mind waves are simply working at an extremely low rate.

Used in this context, meditation is not a verb. It is not something you "do." It is a state you enter into.

Think of it this way. You can consciously raise your right hand. You can deliberately close your eyes. But you cannot intentionally fall asleep right at this moment. You can prepare for sleep. But sleep is not something you "do." It is a state change—your consciousness transitions from one state to another. The practices that precede sleep are (1) lying down, (2) closing your eyes, and (3) getting comfortable. You don't "do" sleep. You lie down. Then sleep comes.

In the same way, practices that precede meditation are (1) relaxation and (2) concentration. You don't "do" meditation. You sit still, relax and concentrate. Then the meditative state comes. When people use the term "meditation" like a verb—i.e., "to meditate"—they usually refer to the practices that precede the state of meditation.

Block 1) Relaxation

A relaxed body enables the mind to become focused. Your goal is to use one or all of the following methods to reach a state where the body is completely still and relaxed and stay in that state for ten to fifteen minutes at least once before adding the next block.

Achieving this may take anywhere from a couple of attempts to a couple of months, depending on your current state of physical tension.

The Relaxation Pose

One of the main differences between relaxation and meditation is that the state of alertness required for meditation is not needed for relaxation. Therefore, lying down is preferable when relaxing, while sitting is imperative when practicing meditation.

Use the following guidelines:

- Lie on your back on a semi-hard surface. The surface may increase tension if too soft or too hard.
- For comfort, place a small pillow under your head and roll a blanket under your

knees for lower back support (both are optional).

- Keep your spine relatively straight and your head centered.
- Allow your feet to part, and point your toes away from the body. This will relax the legs and the hips.
- Your hands point slightly away from your body, and your palms face up. This is comfortable for ninety percent of people, whereas some find it more comfortable to have the palms facing towards the body or, in a few cases, facing down.
- Once you are lying still, you may want to move your shoulder blades apart or together gently and your hips up or down into a more comfortable position.

Use this posture to practice the following relaxation techniques.

Note: If your body is very tense or restless, it can be beneficial to do deep breathing or physical exercises, such as walking or stretching, before attempting to relax.

Relaxation Techniques

Try each technique as a standalone practice; then, experiment with combinations. For beginners, shorter and more frequent practices are better. Start with five to ten minutes, down to two minutes. To begin with, regularity is more important than the length of time. Slowly work your way up to the goal of being utterly relaxed for ten to fifteen minutes.

Tense and Release

Engaging the body is the simplest form of relaxation. It also helps beginners feel like they are "doing" something. Tensing the muscles combines surface tension with deeper muscle tension so that when you release, you release both the conscious tension you created and the underlying tension that was already there.

You can either (1) tense all the muscles of the body at the same time and then relax completely or (2) tense one body part at a time and then relax. Tensing all the muscles is faster, but tensing one muscle group at a time brings deeper relaxation. Inhale when you tense and exhale when you relax. If you plan to tense the entire body, repeat the exercise two to three times for maximum effect.

Try the following sequence if you plan to tense one muscle group at a time.

- Right leg
- Left leg
- Buttocks
- Abdomen (inhale and expand the belly, exhale and relax)
- Chest (inhale and expand the chest, exhale and relax)
- Arms (raise them slightly and make fists, then spread the fingers and relax)
- Face

Experiment with how long you hold the tension in each muscle group (or the entire body).

Deep Breathing

Using breathing techniques allows you to relax anywhere and anytime. When combined with the relaxation pose, the benefits are multiplied.

First, you need to understand that deep breathing is not breathing into your belly but deeper into your lungs, pushing the diaphragm down and expanding your belly. Air in your stomach causes belching, while air deep in your lungs is nourishing and calming.

When you inhale, expand your belly as much as you can. Then expand your chest area while keeping the shoulders relaxed. When you exhale, relax your chest and abdomen, and try to empty your lungs. Repeat this at least ten times.

If you feel lightheaded, return your breathing to normal.

At first, your breathing may feel tense and uncomfortable. You may be tempted to breathe loudly with vigor. Resist that urge. For calming effects, deep breathing should become slow and rhythmic.

That is why you practice—to slow down your breathing. Try to breathe as slowly as you can, with as little noise as possible.

Mental Relaxation

This is similar to the tense and release exercise. Instead of doing anything physically, you scan your body mentally for tension and relax one body part at a time. Focus on large parts of the body, which takes less time or focus on smaller body parts, which takes more time.

For larger parts, consciously relax your legs, hips, back, and so on.

For smaller parts, consciously relax your toes, soles of your feet, tops of your feet, ankles, shins, calves and so on.

Although this is a semi-concentration exercise, the goal is physical relaxation. Even if your mind wanders after a few body parts, you have achieved your goal if the body becomes relaxed.

Measurements for Relaxation

Relaxation is a state between waking and sleeping. Therefore you can have several different experiences when relaxing, all of them beneficial. Here are some measurements to help.

First, your body needs to be mostly still. That is the most important measurement. Yes, mostly still, because sometimes there are slight unconscious movements of the fingers, toes and eyes as the body is ridding itself of tension. However, if you start consciously moving body parts—rolling your head, moving feet or hands—that is a sign that you are not relaxing.

Second, allow your mind to flow freely. If your mind becomes obsessed with one thought or idea, you are not relaxing. But, if your mind flows freely from one thought to another, like when you are dreaming, you are also relaxing. You neither need to put a leash on your mind nor do you have to empty your mind to relax.

Third, you feel better afterward than you did before. With practice, relaxation should increase energy, and you should feel better. The exception is that when you begin to relax regularly, you may feel more tired. That is your body asking for more rest. Keep relaxing and you will gain energy.

Music or No Music?

Relaxation techniques can be used without music. All you need is your body, mind and a quiet place. However, quiet places are increasingly hard to come by almost anywhere in the world. When you can't find a quiet place, use music, white noise, or nature sounds to drown out ambient sounds. If you prefer music, the soundtrack should be instrumental and as neutral as possible.

Practice and Personalization

- First, try each technique at least two or three times. Get a first-hand experience of how they make you feel. Take notes.
- Second, combine two, three, or even all of the techniques based on your preferences.
- Third, set up a practice schedule. Practice anywhere from 3 to 6 times a week. Your primary goal is to create a habit.
- Fourth, practice until you easily reach a relaxed state and stay in that state for 10 to 15 minutes continuously. Then add the second block.

Block 2) The Alertness Pose

Your spine needs to be upright for the nervous system to stay awake and alert. That is the most important aspect of the meditation pose. Everything else is minor in comparison.

If you sit on a chair, sit at the front of the seat with your spine erect.

If you sit cross-legged on the floor—not necessary, but beneficial for those who can— keep a small pillow under your tailbone to keep your spine straight.

Another helpful tip is to keep your knees below your hips. This will aid circulation.

Once your spine is upright and your body still, relax. Relax your arms in your lap or on your knees. Relax your shoulders. Relax your torso as much as you can without slumping. Relax your neck without your head rolling forward, backward or sideways. Relax your legs, feet and so on. Relax every single muscle you are not using.

The pose may take some time to master. Sometimes, all you can do for an entire session is adjust your body until it is comfortable—over and over again. That is a valuable practice in itself. The body needs training to stay still, the same as the mind.

Block 3) Concentration

Any concentrated mental activity or directed stream of consciousness falls into the concentration category. Whether you are remaining alert (mindfulness), focusing on a single thought or phrase (mantra), or mentally exploring the inner world (visualization), all are forms of concentration.

Concentration is the doorway through which the meditative state becomes available. Two concentration exercises are most likely to bring about the meditative state. One is focusing on a word or phrase. The other is alert awareness or relaxed concentration.

The difference between the two can be explained like this. If you were looking at a *Where is Waldo?* picture, concentration would mean looking for Waldo and staying focused on Waldo when you find him. Aware alertness would mean allowing your mind to focus on the entire picture. If your mind latched onto specifics, you would practice letting go, allowing it to wander around in the picture instead.

a) Focus on a Word or Phrase

Focusing on a word or phrase is the most common concentration method and has been taught throughout history as a meditation practice, often with religious connotations. Modern research has found that any word or phrase will do. Still, some research suggests that people who use a word or phrase with personal meaning are likelier to stick with their meditation practice.

When you focus on a word or phrase, the mind slows down and gradually drowns out continuous mental chatter. A big part of using this method is being okay with the fact that the mind will wander. Wandering is the nature of the mind. The wandering mind is not disturbing the practice (as many novices think when they begin). Gently struggling with the mind is the practice.

Single words like *Love*, *Light*, *Calm*, *Peace* and *Relax* are good examples of focus words. Religions, such as Hinduism and Buddhism, have a solid meditative foundation and offer a variety of words and phrases (mantras) to choose from. People with a Christian background may want to select phrases like *Thy Will Be Done* or *Maranatha* (Aramaic for "Come Lord"). Atheists and agnostics can choose any word or phrase that speaks to their peaceful mental side. The goal is to find a word or phrase you resonate with personally because you will be repeating the word or phrase mentally for years to come if you stick with the practice.

When you have chosen a word and are ready to begin, sit in the alertness pose and relax. Once your body is still, repeat the word or phrase in your mind, either continuously or in rhythm with your breathing. When your mind wanders, gently bring your attention back to the word or phrase without judgment. Begin with five minutes of concentration, and then work up to ten to twenty minutes.

b) Alert Awareness

Imagine sitting on the porch of a coffee house in a busy city, relaxed, taking in the entire scenery, the whole picture. You are a passive observer, not involved in anything happening. That is aware alertness in a nutshell. You close your eyes and passively observe your mind, non-judgmentally and without getting caught up in any thought.

The key to alert awareness is letting go and not allowing one thought or image to dominate your mind for an extended period. Whether the thought is pleasurable or painful, it doesn't matter; let it go and allow your mind to be alert to the entirety of what you experience.

Using this method, your focus is on letting go and passively observing; that is the concentration part of the practice. Although different from the previous concentration exercise, the effects are similar. Start with five minutes and work up to ten to twenty minutes.

Personalization & Practice

- First, try each concentration practice for a week for a minimum of five to ten minutes. Journal about your experiences.
- Second, choose one of the practices or combine practices (for example, starting with a word or phrase and then retreating to alert awareness halfway through your practice).

- Third, continue your chosen practice and learn to discern the meditative state (next block).

Block 4) Uncover the State

As previously stated, meditation is not something that you "do." It is a state you transition into when the circumstances are right. Practicing relaxation and concentration creates the right circumstances. Now, all you need to do is notice the meditative state so that you can enjoy it when it comes.

At this point, many people need clarification. They think that the practices explained thus far are "meditation" because they confuse practices with the state of being.

"Meditation is like dreamless sleep awake."

That is how you discern; by contemplating the definition.

When you practice concentration, and your mind becomes still, even for a brief time, that is meditation. Those moments of stillness are not a distraction from the practice. They are meditation.

"Dreamless sleep awake."

That is meditation.

Other words that describe the state are…
…peaceful
…blissful
…vast
…calm
…clear

Practice Produces Experiences

Imagine a time before you had chocolate. Going to lectures about chocolate would have been interesting. Reading about chocolate might have increased your appetite. But only tasting chocolate would have made you understand how good chocolate can be.

To begin with, the meditative state may come for a few moments at a time. With practice, you will enter it more often and for longer periods.

Enjoy Each Step

It is human nature to be impatient. We all want results. We want them fast. But, when practicing meditation, impatience is a hindrance.

- Instead of waiting for the meditative state and being frustrated every time you don't achieve it, learn to enjoy the benefits of each progressive step.

- Enjoy the benefits of physical relaxation. Even if you do nothing else, a regular relaxation practice can do wonders.

- Be happy when you can sit still for a few minutes. Taming the body to be still is an important step.

- And even if you sit still and keep thinking about everything in your life, be happy about that as well. You can solve many of your problems that way.

These steps are simple. They should be simple. Simplicity is everywhere in nature, and meditation is a natural state. Meditation is a state of peaceful equilibrium that is always available.

Not the Same as Laziness

A common misconception states that mindfulness, especially meditation, is the same as laziness. I want to explain why it's not the same and illustrate how you can tell the difference.

Let's start with a joke.

Two older gentlemen meet in the street.

"How are you?" says one.

"Well, thank you. And you?" says the other.

"I am also well. Any news on your son? Is he still living at home?"

"Yes, but he's meditating now."

"Meditating? Is that any good?"

"I guess so. It beats sitting around doing nothing, right?"

Doing Nothing?

The joke accomplishes two things. It's funny, and it points to a double-edged perception that people have about meditation. From the outside, meditation is just sitting and doing nothing, making it hard to tell laziness apart from a mindful moment. How can we tell which is which?

Three States of Water

In Eastern traditions, energy is often described as three states of water; swamp, raging river and deep lake. Swamp energy is stagnant. River energy is forceful and erratic. Lake energy is calm and powerful. From the outside, a swamp and a lake appear similar, but the difference couldn't be more dramatic underneath the surface. One has depth and clarity; the other is murky and sluggish.

Mindful or Lazy?

Comparing a mindful moment with laziness is similar to comparing a lake and a swamp. On the surface, both appear identical. The body is still, and the face is calm. The inner states, however, are far removed from one another. Laziness is devoid of energy. Mindfulness is full of calm energy. The outward appearances make it difficult to discern between the two, but the inner feelings are distinct and relatively easy to measure. The critical question is: How do you feel afterward?

The Hot Bath Example

Those who enjoy a hot bath will know from experience that a Goldilocks approach is needed for the best results. The activity is the same, but the outcomes vary depending on how long you stay in the water. If you stay too short, you don't get to a state of relaxation. If you stay in too long, you will be tired for the rest of the day.

How You Feel is a Measurement

A quick way to measure the mindfulness of a moment is this. If any activity leaves you feeling satisfied, calmer and full of energy, you've experienced a mindful moment. If the activity leaves you feeling lethargic and depleted, you have succumbed to laziness.

It is possible to see how much energy other people have after certain activities, but the reference point of feelings is mainly for you, the individual. Use it to gauge which activities are mindful and which ones are energy-depleting. Sometimes you need a change of activity; other times, all you need to do is calibrate the amount of time you spend in relaxation or meditation, similar to what you'd do in a hot bath.

p.s. For the record, let me say that I am not demonizing laziness. It is part of the natural cycle of being human. We all fall into that energy from time to time, and laziness has its benefits; it's just not a good place to live.

Plan or Be in the Moment?

"Do you plan everything or live in the moment?"

I was at an Indian restaurant in Austin recently when I overheard this question.

I didn't say anything to the couple playing twenty questions, but internally I answered: "Both. There is no paradox. One aids the other."

Symbiotic Relationship

As a student of both mindfulness and goal setting, I've realized that there is a symbiotic relationship between planning and living in the moment. The better I plan, the more I can let go of my thoughts about the future and live in the moment, focusing on one task at a time to the exclusion of everything else. The more I focus and live in the moment, the easier it is to plan.

Wasn't Always This Way

I ascribed fully to the "live in the moment" paradigm in my early twenties. Planning was for geeks and business people. I was creative and needed to be spontaneous. I felt like planning would stifle my creativity and limit my choices.

However, when the reality of life set in, bills to pay, food to prepare, and people to take care of, I found that I was living more and more in the future. Because I refused to plan, I constantly needed to remind myself of upcoming tasks, work hours, social gatherings, shopping lists, etc. The list in my head often seemed endless. My mind was so crowded that creativity was stifled.

Finding Balance

It took a few years to find a balance. Sometimes I became so enthralled with the planning and goal-setting process that I forgot to live in the moment. Other times I was entirely in the moment. Future orientation seemed redundant, unhelpful even.

The process I've settled on is simple. I have an overall direction—a purpose of serving—

and then I set goals for the year, plan each month at the end of the preceding month, each week at the end of the preceding week, and each day at the end of the preceding day. In the long run, this process has saved me both time and energy.

Mindfulness is layered on top. Once I have a plan, I do one thing at a time and do not think ahead to what comes next. My list takes care of that. This approach frees up tremendous brain space. Most importantly, it allows me to settle into each moment and focus on the task, whether working, family time, or something else.

Results Speak for Themselves

On the productivity side, the results speak for themselves. I've managed to write thirty books in twenty years, run a yoga studio, be a sought-after speaker, coach people, study to become an interfaith minister and be the primary caretaker for my two children.

The mindfulness side is harder to quantify. My ability to focus is unquestioned, but I would be lying if I said that living in the moment has always produced peace of mind. Some moments are challenging. That's life. What mindfulness has done is allow me to face each moment fully without the need for numbing. That is a quantifiable plus for someone who ran away from difficulties and used substances to aid in that escape.

Intertwine, Don't Choose

My point is straightforward: You don't have to choose between planning and living in the moment. By intertwining these two essential aspects, your life will be enriched. It's not always easy, but you will be present and productive.

Motivation

"Man, alone, has the power to transform his thoughts into physical reality; man, alone, can dream and make his dreams come true."

Napoleon Hill

People Don't Want Change

People say they want change.
They ask for change, demand it even.
People go to great lengths for promises of change.
When they get it, however, not everyone likes the outcome.
Coronavirus changed the world.
Most of us didn't like that one bit.
Asking for change is redundant.
Change is a constant.
Things change.
That is the nature of the world.
What most people want are improvements.
They want their lives to improve.
Their fortunes to improve.
Society to improve.
When people ask for change, that is what they get, change.
Maybe it's time to stop asking for change.
Instead, ask for improvements.
Work toward them.
Who knows, it might work.

The Goal-Setting Process

Imagine a new ship that has just arrived at the harbor. It's technically more advanced than other ships in its fleet. It has powerful engines, better steering, and the navigation system communicates with the most advanced satellites.

Now imagine that someone decided to test drive the ship by giving it full throttle without coordinates or a crew aboard.

The ship wouldn't get far.

If it got out of the harbor, it would likely spin in circles, bump into other ships, become stranded, or be at the mercy of waves and winds.

The same is true of people. Without a clear direction, people can be swept away by prevailing winds or circle around in confusion.

The Journey is Success

Earl Nightingale defined success as *"the progressive realization toward a worthy ideal or goal."* His definition claimed that anyone taking steps towards a goal is already successful.

This means that if someone dreams of owning a corner store, that person is successful from the first day of putting aside money for that store; if someone dreams of becoming a chemistry professor, that person is already successful when signing up for the class; if someone dreams of becoming a writer, every written sentence delivers instant success; if someone wants to become a better parent and starts rearranging priorities, success is achieved.

You are successful all the days that you take deliberate steps toward the goals and dreams you have set for yourself.

Two Things to Know About Goal Setting

1. People who write down their goals usually achieve them in a shorter period than those with an unclear vision of what they want.

2. Taking steps towards one goal opens doors to other possibilities that might otherwise have remained invisible.

The second principle is called the corridor principle. A person standing at the end of a corridor, refusing to walk, will not see doors open on either side. But a person that moves and starts walking down the aisle will be exposed to new opportunities. The person who moves can change direction anytime in light of new information or options. In contrast, the person standing still will not be exposed to anything new, stranded in a place of indecision.

Ready, Fire, Aim is not only a book title but a popular term with certain self-development teachers. It points to a flaw in people's thinking in general. Many spend so much time aiming that they never fire. But goals are like missiles; their aim can be adjusted once fired.

Three Common Problems

There are three common problems related to goal setting.

- One is buying into other people's ideas of success. Many people have climbed the ladder of success only to find that it is leaning against the wrong building. Make sure that your goals reflect your dreams.

- Another is an imbalance between being at peace and wanting to grow. Growth mode is proactive and can be pretty stressful. Being at peace is lovely, but staying there too long can degenerate into lethargy. The aim is to find a balance between the desire to grow and moments of mindfulness.

- The third is unrealistic deadlines. There are few unrealistic goals but many unrealistic deadlines. If the deadline is too close, people fail because they can't finish what they started. If the deadline is too far away, people won't generate the energy they need to act. Learn to set deadlines that generate energy while allowing enough time to finish the job.

Goal and Dream Exercise

The following goal and dream exercise is one way to set goals. It can be done in an hour or over a few days. The exercise encourages long-term thinking and imagination, the creation of short-term goals, and setting action steps in motion.

Step 1) If All My Dreams Come True

Dreams generate a special kind of passion and willpower, both of which will help people navigate the seas of life. Dreams should not be confused with daydreams or thoughts of escape. A dream is more like a magnet and works like the North Star did for the ancient seafarers. To create your dream, answer this question:

"What will my life look like in 10 years if all my dreams come true?"

Let go of limitations and let your imagination run free. What would you wish for if you had a magic wand and all your wishes could come true?

Here are questions to help you get started:

- Which character traits do you wish to possess in ten years?
- What vices are you free from?
- What is your level of education?

- What experiences do you have?
- Where in the world are you if all your dreams come true?
- Who are the people you are with?
- What are you doing?
- What do you possess?
- Who are you serving and helping?

By allowing yourself to dream, you are painting a picture with words, conjuring up a compelling vision that will drive your everyday actions.

Dreaming does not guarantee anything, but it is an essential first step.

Step 2) Create 10 Goals

Write ten goals for the next twelve months. Make sure the goals align with your dream or vision; they should be stepping stones toward your imagined life.

Your goals will likely fall into two categories, lifestyle or outcome.

Lifestyle: If your goal is to include exercise and meditation in your routine, you will have achieved those goals once the activities have become habits and you no longer have to think about them.

Outcome: Be specific. Write the number of pounds you plan to gain or lose, the amount of money you are going to earn or save, the deadlines for your project, etc. Each outcome goal must be measurable and achievable.

For goals to be goals, you have to do something you haven't done before, something new or something you plan to do better. Writing a to-do list of things you already know you can achieve is not goal setting; it's planning.

Step 3) Take Action

Time to take action. Read through your goals and dreams and incorporate them into your daily routine. The goals you've set for yourself need your attention. Look at them every day. Write them and rewrite them. Turn them into affirmations and constantly chant them. Most importantly, do something every day that moves you forward.

Now, list new things you may need to learn to achieve your goals. Be open and attentive. Once goals are at the forefront of your mind, you will start noticing things in your environment that will help you to reach them faster.

List everyone who can help you succeed and enlist their support.

Finally, try only working on ten goals at a time. Once a goal is reached, substitute it with another. That way, you will always have ten goals to work toward.

Ten is a Goldilocks number. Not so many that you'll feel overwhelmed, not so few that you'll feel bored.

Motivation and Excitement

Pumped up! That's how many people think of motivation. High energy. Go-getters. In comparison, most people appear unmotivated. They exclaim, "I wish I were that motivated. I just can't seem to get pumped."

The problem is that motivation is different from excitement. Not knowing the difference between the two can cause all kinds of issues. Allow me to explain.

Excitement is Short-Lived

I love getting excited about things. That burst of energy and high intensity makes me feel like I can do anything.

Still, I've learned that living at that level is unsustainable. Excitement is short-lived. It fizzles out. The feeling is great while it lasts, but I can't count on it.

Like an Undercurrent

In comparison, well-developed motivation is like an undercurrent. It pulls me in the right direction even when I try to swim against it. Motivation comes from a deep psychological source. It speaks to my values. Who I am and what I need to live a fulfilled life.

Developing Motivation

As a personal coach, I spend a lot of time helping people uncover their motivations and create an undercurrent. Getting there often takes time.

I've found that the clearer people are about why they want something, the more motivated they are. The critical question is 'why?' Then ask 'why' again. And again. Often more than five times.

Motivation Drives Behavior

All the big and important things in life—education, relationships, career advancement, spiritual growth, and physical wellness—depend on consistent long-term action. Motivation drives that behavior; getting up, working out, working hard... consistently doing what is difficult.

What's Wrong With Excitement?

There is nothing wrong with excitement. It's just not the same as motivation. Short bursts of energy are great if you are playing American football and need a first down, but excitement is not enough for the big goals in life. We can't depend on emotional highs to sustain us.

Understanding the Difference

The difference between motivation and excitement is evident when you stop and think about it. Yet, it is not always clear when you are in the moment. That is why it is important to understand the difference.

Personally, I've learned to use excitement to my benefit when it aligns with my motivations. I often make tremendous progress in a short period when I am pumped up. But I've also learned to be suspicious of excitement and not make big decisions when riding high.

Most importantly, I've learned that the most excited person is not always the most motivated one in the room, even when that person is me.

No Time Management

The title makes a bold statement. But it's true. There is no such thing as time management. Time passes. Period. No mere mortal can change that. All we can do is learn how to manage ourselves within the context of time.

The Hour Glass

I fell for the concept of time management back in the late nineties when I was starting my professional career. The first book I read on the subject was called *The Hourglass*. It offered various suggestions on how to get more done in less time and suggested habits that I still use.

Eat That Frog

Then Brian Tracy came along. *Eat That Frog* is still the best book on the topic I've ever seen. It is based on a brilliant premise. If the worst thing you have to do during the day is to eat a slimy frog, it's probably best to do that first. Otherwise, having to do it later takes focus away from other tasks and causes stress. The frog is symbolic of our biggest and most important tasks.

More Time?

I learned so much that I offered various time management courses in the early 2000s and hammered on the term as if it were possible.

Pretty soon, however, I noticed a common theme. People kept telling me that they needed more time. I always responded the same: "We all have the same amount of time. Everyone gets the same 24 hours." But it didn't dawn on me what that really meant until later.

The Myth of Time Management

Awakening happens in the funniest ways. Because I had been introduced to time management early, I never doubted it for a second. I took it for granted that time management was possible. It took hundreds of hours of teaching the topic and getting feedback from dozens until I realized the folly of my ways. People were not managing their time. They were managing themselves.

Self-Management

That's what every so-called time management lesson is; *self-management*. We learn to manage ourselves, including our habits and tendencies, while increasing our ability to prioritize. Over time, we become more effective. What used to take a long time is now quicker and easier. As a result, we get more done. Time was never managed in that process. It kept passing. We learned to manage ourselves.

Important Distinction

Why is this important? Because it changes the locus of control. Most people perceive time as an external force. Labeling their efforts as time management gives them a false sense of control over that external force. But labeling the same activities as self-management transfers control to the individual. I control what I do with myself within the context of time.

This is no mere exercise in semantics. I've experienced it myself and seen it with my own eyes.

The Price of Anything

Henry David Thoreau was a 19th Century American philosopher and journalist. He wrote that the price of anything is the amount of life you are willing to exchange for it. How we spend our time is how we spend our life. That is what time is; life.

So, here's the challenge.

Try replacing the term time management with *self-management*. See how that changes your perspective. You can engage in all the great 'time management' activities you've learned. Just call them by their real name.

Permission to Dream

Lately, I've been working with several clients who've been going through transitions. Whether people are moving from the carefree twenties to the responsible thirties, shifting focus from one life purpose to another, switching jobs, recovering from a slump in their forties or reinventing life in retirement, I've encouraged everyone to pause, put aside limiting beliefs, and allow themselves to dream.

Giving People Permission

Some give me confused looks. Others exclaim, "Am I allowed to do that?" Why? Because most people live their lives by putting their heads down. They work, raise a family, and pay bills. Their lives are busy, busy, busy. There is no time for dreaming. When I give them permission—something which was not mine to give—it can take them a while to accept and give themselves permission.

Creating a Safe Space

For most, dreaming is not easy. Some have tossed the activity aside as a childish fantasy. Others have had their dreams crushed and feel insecure about even allowing themselves to think that way. Adding to the complexity, most people fear how others will react. They've had experiences where they shared dreams and were immediately told to get their heads out of the clouds.

For the reasons mentioned above—and many more—it is imperative to create a safe space to dream in and be selective about with whom to share the dreams. When people feel safe and secure, they are willing to let go of limitations.

Generates Motivation

When done correctly, dreaming can become a gravitational force, an unending source of motivation, a mental picture that will keep you going even when you don't feel like getting out of bed.

Will You Allow Yourself to Dream?

Most days are not for dreaming. They are for doing. But now and then, it is good to look up from the toil of everyday life and see the horizon. A dream is like a mountain top. In the same way you would look to the mountain top while climbing a mountain and then put your head down and take one step at a time, having a compelling vision for the future helps you get through challenging days. You will know what you are working toward.

Without a Vision?

A well-known scripture verse reminds us that *people perish where there is no vision*. If that is true about societies, isn't that true about individuals?

Having a vision gives life purpose and meaning. It drives good behavior and helps people overcome obstacles. If you do not have a vision, permit yourself to dream. Who knows? It may become a reality.

Self-Confidence and Trust

Have you ever said you were going to do something and then found an excuse not to do it? Of course, you have. Welcome to the club. Most of us go back on our word regularly. We call it being human. We say one thing, then do another.

One of my seminar attendees told me he'd made a new year's resolution: "I am going to start smoking, get drunk as often as I can and cheat on my wife on a regular basis. Since I know that I always go in the opposite direction of my new year's resolutions, it will be a good year."

This man had become so distrustful of his intentions that he decided to use that disbelief to his advantage. It didn't work.

Sadly, once people get used to the fact that they usually don't do what they say they're going to do, feelings of self-esteem, self-confidence and self-worth begin to diminish. This is because being untruthful is universally scorned. If people would constantly go back on their word, we'd lose respect for them and start avoiding their presence. Similarly, if we deceive ourselves, it perpetuates feelings of distrust and disrespect.

The ways out of this dilemma are to stop promising too much or do more of what you have said you will do.

Definition of Self-Confidence

That brings me to my favorite two-phrase definition of self-confidence.

- I trust myself to face life's challenges.
- I trust myself to follow my dreams and goals.

When faced with obstacles, self-confident people think: "I will find a way to solve this. I will find a way through. If I can't find a solution, I will find someone to help me." One could say that the pinnacle of self-confidence is reached when a person can say, "I don't know, I need help," without feeling any shame. Self-confident people also follow their goals and dreams. They trust themselves to learn and do what is needed.

Self-confidence is not fixed. People are not born with a set amount. Confidence can be gained and lost. And it can differ between the roles you play; swell in one area of life and be lacking in another.

What if You've Lost It?

What if you've broken so many of your promises that you no longer trust yourself? First, know that you're not alone. Second, know that if you decide to rebuild trust, it takes time.

Let's put this idea in perspective. If someone has betrayed you repeatedly, you won't automatically start believing them just because they promise to do or not to do something. You'll need proof.

The same goes for trust in yourself. You will only start believing what you say or think once you start seeing results.

Instead of making lofty promises, begin with little things. Make small promises to yourself and keep them. Once you keep your word on the small stuff, you can promise bigger things.

Trust Yourself

Having self-confidence is not about being better than anyone else. It's about trusting yourself to face life and to develop and enhance your gifts and talents.

Cure for Co-Dependency

Co-dependency revolves around the sentence: *"I am not enough."* A co-dependent person needs another to validate their worth, feelings, ideas and existence.

This expresses itself in two ways.

People try to control and manipulate their surroundings on one end or bend over backward to make others feel good on the other, their reasoning being, "I can't feel good if you don't feel good."

Peach or Coconut?

Would you rather be a peach or a coconut?

Before you answer, consider this.

A peach is beautiful on the outside, luscious and attractive, but bruises easily and is hard on the inside. A person like a peach always tries to look good and be good to everyone but gets harder on the inside, constantly feeling more bitter and guilty. Telltale sentences include: "I do everything for everyone. Why doesn't anyone do anything for me?" It's easy to become hard on the inside if you're waiting for the world to repay your kindness quid pro quo.

Peaches abound in conventional caretaker industries; nurses, kindergarten teachers, coaches, yoga teachers, and social workers. I have met many peaches in my workshops over the years; heck, I was one. They are good people trying to make a difference. Unfortunately, many have put on masks of gentleness, trying to please everyone they meet (which is simply impossible).

That's where the coconut comes in. It's hard and uninviting on the outside, but once you get past the shell, you encounter a haven of superb nourishment. A person who is more like a coconut may not bend over backward to make sure everyone likes her, but the people she lets through her shell are bathed with the same love and attention she nourishes herself with on the inside. The coconut is a reservoir. Internal feelings of self-worth and service orientation expand to the outside.

Life-Changing Affirmation

Having seen the limits of living like a peach, I have chosen to be more like a coconut. The transition took a lot of work. I needed to repeat the following affirmation near-daily for years and have since taught it to thousands of people with good results. It goes like this:

I am not going to like everyone,
not everyone is going to like me,
and that is OK.

Most people are quick to agree with the first part, that they will not like everyone. What naturally follows, however, is that not everyone is going to like them. That's harder to swallow.

"But I'm so likable!" people exclaim.

When I remind them (gently) that sometimes they don't like others who have done nothing to deserve it, they go, "Oh, you mean people feel the same way about me?" Yes. It's a truth that, once accepted, makes life much easier. You have to remind yourself that it's OK.

Allergy Medicine

I wish I could tell you that feelings of co-dependency will go away completely, but the treatment I offer is more like allergy medicine than corrective surgery. Repeated regularly, the affirmation will lessen the feelings, managing the problem rather than removing it. Still, that alone can be life-changing.

Navigating Transitions

We all go through transitions in life. The most common ones include childhood to puberty, school to work, single to married, self-care to parenthood, working to stay-at-home, working to retirement, and married to divorced.

Rules No Longer Apply

What all of these transitions have in common is that the rules people used to live by no longer apply.

Some reject that. They try to hold onto the previous stage, refusing to change their behavior. Sometimes the outcome is mildly amusing—like when someone resists growing up—other times devastating.

Life Moves in One Direction

In truth, life moves in one direction, *forward*. The better prepared we are for the inevitability of change, the more we can adapt to new circumstances, and the easier our journey. Accepting this is a great beginning.

Event + Response = Outcome

Jack Canfield used the above formula in all of his talks back in the day. He reminded his audiences that outcomes in life are based on life events and our responses to them. When events change, we must adapt our responses.

It's true. Our lives are a *combination* of events and responses. Some people only blame events and outside forces for their misfortunes in life. Others think that everything happens because of how they think and act.

The reality is that it takes both.

Transition Examples

Several of my clients are going through transitions. One woman lost her husband in a tragic accident and is reinventing her life. Another woman is fast approaching retirement and hasn't thought about what life will look like after she stops working. And one man I worked with used to be an entrepreneur, retired, but couldn't get himself to stop doing business, even though he didn't need the money. Depending on their circumstances, we are working to find out how they can adapt and flourish in their new roles. Here are some of the questions we are using to help.

What are the New Rules?

How is this era of life different from the previous one? What are the new rules you need to live by? For instance, the biggest difference from childhood to adulthood is increased responsibility.

Granted, sometimes we don't know what the new rules are. Last year, I learned about the happiness curve. It describes a measurable dip in happiness between forty and fifty. I wish I'd known about that earlier. Thankfully, I can now help others navigate that time more efficiently.

How Do You Need to Adapt?

Events have changed. How are you going to adapt to your new situation? Some transitions are foreseeable. You can prepare. Others happen out of the blue. Oh, and sometimes people pretend that a foreseeable transition is not coming, and it, predictably, catches them off guard.

What is the Same About You?

No matter the transitions, you are still you. What is it that remains the same throughout all transitions? What is good that you want to hold onto no matter what? Knowing the answer will help you navigate new terrain by giving you a centering point.

Have Your Values Changed?

When I was younger, my values were decidedly different. My main focus was to have fun. As I aged, my focus shifted from myself to helping others. Whenever I can assist another human being, it makes me feel valuable. What are your values? Which ones have stayed the same? Which ones have changed? Again, knowing this will help you find balance when the new terrain knocks you sideways.

Do You Need to Learn New Skills?

What skills would help you during the transition you are going through or the ones you anticipate? The skills category can include anything from the tangible, such as learning how to sew or woodwork, to the intangible, such as interpersonal skills, goal setting, time management, and mindfulness. My friend, Marc Miller at Career Pivot, explains that as careers advance or change, we need to be willing to pivot. That may include learning new skills. The same can be true of other areas, such as relationships.

Steadiness and Adaptability

As you can see, the two most important things you can foster if you want to move through transitions more easily are *steadiness* and *adaptability*. Knowing who you are, what you can do, and what you value will provide you with steadiness. Accepting transitions as a part of life will help you adapt.

Good Intent, Bad Habits

Imagine this. You're a teenager trying to create a new habit. You've decided to jump out of bed every time the alarm rings. But you don't. Day after day, the alarm goes off, you hit snooze, and your parents wake you up yelling and screaming because you are late. You tell yourself (and them): "Tomorrow. I'll do it tomorrow." But it doesn't change.

Creating a Bad Habit

In this scenario, you've created a bad habit while trying to instill a new habit. You habitually snooze and wait to be rescued. Your parents could teach you a hard lesson and stop waking you up, but that's not the point of this example. The point is that because you kept trying and failing, you created a bad habit.

Repetition

Habit formation depends on repetition. The more often you do something, the likelier it is to stick as a habit. That's human psychology 101. What many don't seem to realize, however, is that unsuccessful repetition also counts. If you do something over and over the wrong way, you learn the wrong way, and that sticks.

Motivate Yourself or Stop

You can do two things to ensure this does not happen.

The first is to make sure that the new habit you are trying to instill is something you want. Look at your motivations (both negative and positive). What does it give you? What does it save you from? What will your life look like if you succeed?

The second is to stop. Yes, stop trying. I've found that it is better to eliminate a habit formation attempt than to keep trying and failing.

In the earlier example, the teenager might first look at reasons for wanting to wake up to an alarm clock, considering both the positive—such as autonomy—and the negative—such as being late or yelled at. Here is the hard part, however. If the teenager is not motivated to change, it is better to halt the experiment and try later than to keep reinforcing the bad habit of not waking up to an alarm.

Habits in Your Life?

Think about your life. Have you created any bad habits because you were trying to instill new ones? What were they? How did that affect your life? Are you still a slave to those habits, or have you broken free? What would it take to create new habits?

Honest self-reflection about this topic can be liberating. I've worked with countless adults who have re-imagined their relationship with habits after undergoing a similar exercise. Some have discovered compelling reasons to create habits that eluded them. Others have realized that they never wanted the habit in the first place; it was just something they thought they should be doing.

Clarity in Habit Formation

People are what they consistently do. Habits control their lives in many ways. Some habits can be changed. Other habits can be created. Yet others are so deeply ingrained that people must learn how to live with them. This means that the more clarity you have concerning your habits, the better off you are.

Get Help If You Need It

Every coach would be out of a job if this were easy. Uncovering motivation alone can be a hefty task that requires mirroring and support. Whether you work with a friend, family member, spiritual adviser, coach or someone else, make sure you get help. Habits are too important to be left up to chance.

Self-Reliant Goals

People sometimes set themselves up for failure because they create goals that rely on circumstances, events and other people; in essence, all the things that they cannot control. Naturally, no person is an island. We live in communion with the Earth and all its inhabitants. Still, there are ways to make goals more self-reliant by making them dependent on personal input rather than other-centered outcomes.

Speaker Who Wanted to Motivate

Ten years ago, I worked with a man preparing to make a big speech to hundreds of people. I asked him what his goal was.

"I want to motivate people and make them feel inspired," he said.

"Then you will fail," I answered flatly. "You cannot control how other people feel."

Before we move on to my proposed solution, please think about that for a moment. None of us can control *how other people feel.*

But… we can influence them with how we feel and with *our behavior.* So, that's what I asked the speaker-in-preparation to do.

"If you want to motivate, be motivated. Tell the best stories you know about motivation. Show the audience how motivation has changed your life. And, if you want to inspire, be inspired."

He took my advice, and the talk was a success. Later, he told me that the biggest lesson he took away from our preparation was: "The more I influence myself, the better I can influence others."

Selling Pots and Pans

Let's take another example. Imagine a person who works selling pots and pans from house to house. An 'other-reliant goal' for this person would be to say: "I am going to sell 50 pots and pans." Some days, they'll hit the number; other days, they won't. The salesperson cannot control how many pots and pans other people buy.

However, if the salesperson decides, "I am going to present the pots and pans in the best possible way, use all the demonstration skills I know, tell stories of how well they have worked for others, listen to concerns and respond in an informative and persuasive manner, and offer the pots and pans for sale more than once because I know that the average person needs to be offered something for sale six times before they make a decision," the goal has become self-reliant.

What Can You Control?

Self-reliant goal-setters ask, "what can I control?" and then focus on those things. Preparation, contribution, mindset, work ethic, effort, emotion, determination and grit are all examples of self-reliance in goal setting. You can't control the outcome, but you can set yourself up for success.

What About Luck?

Let me reiterate; you will need cooperation. Your life does not happen in a vacuum. It is dependent on other human beings. And, like it or not, there is a certain degree of luck involved. Being at the right place at the right time. Knowing the right people. Pessimists may even cry out: "Why bother? The whole thing is stacked against me."

I have a more hopeful view. An old saying goes: *"Luck is when preparedness meets opportunity."* You cannot control opportunity, even if you put yourself in the right spots and cultivate relationships (which you should do, nonetheless), but you can maintain preparedness.

Shifting to Self-Reliance

Try shifting your focus to self-reliance. Set goals that encourage you to do the things that are within your control and focus less on the things you have no direct control over. You will have more success because you will have more control.

Mine Yourself

"How many people here are not using everything they already know how to do?"

This was a question I started asking after years of giving workshops. The reason was simple. Many participants believed they needed to learn something new to advance.

This focus on 'new' overlooked something of importance; what they already knew.

So, I started asking the question. Without exception, everyone raised their hand.

It's true. Every single person in every workshop I offered—hundreds of people— raised their hand to admit that they were only using a fraction of what they already knew. My follow-up question was always the same.

"How would your life be better if you used more of what you already know?"

Light bulbs illuminated as people told me how their life would improve.

Simple Exercise

In response to this near-universal admission, I created a simple exercise in four parts. It goes like this.

Step 1) List what you know how to do. This list can include everything from first grade onward. Don't limit yourself to things that you've done. Everything you've read but haven't acted on counts as something you know, especially if you've ever said: "I know better."

Step 2) List what you are currently doing. Include your job, your health habits, the communication guidelines you follow, and so on. The length of this list will depend on age and experience.

Step 3) Ask: "How would my life improve if I used more of what I know?" Ideally, answering this question will help you make a list of what to do and illustrate how that would improve your life.

Step 4) Make a plan to implement. How can you incorporate more of what you know into your everyday life? Prioritize the list. Add one or two things every month or every other month. It should be easier than implementing something new because this is something you already know.

Increases Self-Reliance

Using this exercise increases self-reliance. Instead of constantly looking outwardly for answers, you will start looking inwardly.

Learning vs Doing Ratios

Too many people have reversed the ratio between learning and doing. They spend inordinate amounts of time listening to podcasts, watching interviews, browsing through YouTube videos, attending classes, reading articles, and participating in workshops, leaping from one to another without pausing to implement. Knowledge increases, but lives don't improve.

New Knowledge is Supplemental

The truth is that all new knowledge is *supplemental*. It adds to what you already know and what you've already experienced. Suppose you keep pushing that aside, wanting to start from ground zero every time. In that case, the learning curve is so steep that the improvements you seek don't materialize (which is another way of saying what I wrote in the previous paragraph).

Trust Yourself More

The bottom line is this. Your life can improve dramatically if you use more of what you already know. The more you mine your knowledge and experience, the more you will trust yourself, and, as I've written before, self-trust leads to self-confidence.

Make Time for the Exercise

Make time for this simple exercise. It can take anywhere from an hour to half a day. It's a small price because I've seen it improve lives before my eyes for both workshop attendees and coaching clients.

Being Hard on Yourself

Most people are too hard on themselves. That is a consensus statement. Friends, family, clients and workshop participants all nod their heads in agreement when someone utters those words. "Yeah, we are too hard on ourselves," they say.

The paradox is that people are also too easy on themselves. They are quick to backtrack on promises surrounding exercise, diet, habit formation, goals, and the list goes on. While people may keep their promises to others, promises they make to themselves get sidelined.

I've learned that there are right circumstances to be hard on yourself—to push through limits—and there are wrong circumstances. Sadly, most people do the opposite of what I am about to propose.

What Most People Do

First, let's take a look at what most people do.

- One, they are hard on themselves emotionally. Their heads are full of self-deprecating thoughts. Their greatest hits include: "I am no good. How could I be so stupid? What is wrong with me? I'm such an idiot." The list goes on. A seminar attendee told me years ago that she never took anything anyone had to say to her personally. Why? Because she had probably said something worse about herself.

- Two, people are soft on themselves physically. They wake up later than planned, throw diet guidelines out the window, don't exercise regularly, and allow other physical self-discipline to slide—all while emotionally bashing themselves.

You can see how unhealthy both behaviors are when spelled out with such clarity. Lack of physical discipline is a health crisis in plain sight. Emotional thrashing leads to anxiety, stress, and various mental health issues.

What I Propose

What I propose is to flip these behaviors. Learn to be harder on yourself physically and take it easy on yourself emotionally. Do things that are good for you physically while at the same time saying no to relentless guilt, shame and self-sabotage.

Most people already possess the lax attitude needed to give themselves an emotional break. Instead of using it for permission to eat more candy, sleep longer or exercise less, the goal would be to shift it to emotions. Take it easy. Relax. Don't be so hard on yourself. Try it the next time your inner critic rears its ugly head.

Being hard on yourself physically means this: Do what you say you are going to do when you say you are going to do it, whether you feel like it or not.

Overriding feelings of lethargy is not easy, so make sure that you have the motivation and a sufficiently low bar. Yes, low bar. I've seen more people self-sabotage by setting the bar too high than I care to remember, myself included. Rather than promising to exercise six times a week, promise three times and stick to it no matter what. If that is still too high, commit to two times. Once you start clearing the bar, make it more difficult and promise more. Success breeds success.

Flip the Switch

If this idea intrigues you, flip the switch. Be hard on yourself physically and take it easy on yourself emotionally. Your every effort will be rewarded.

Self-Worth Affirmations

A healthy sense of self-worth should be innate and unlinked to behavior. Self-worth says: "I have permission to be here. I am worthy no matter what I do."

I was in my early twenties when I was first introduced to this revolutionary idea.

"You mean I am worthy just for living, not because of who I am with or where I work or how people evaluate my actions?"

"Yes," I was told. "All those things can add to your feelings of self-satisfaction and self-confidence, but you are worth being here no matter what you do."

Rising Like the Phoenix

Imagine how many times I had told myself the opposite. And I was not alone. Over the years, I've met hundreds of people who've told me they were engaged in constant negative self-talk. How can we rise from something like that?

Brian Tracy offered a solution during his *Phoenix* seminar, two simple affirmations. The name of the course turned out to be prophetic because afterward, I arose like a phoenix and changed my trajectory in life.

The Rationale

The rationale behind the following two affirmations is simple. If you repeat them often and with emotions (which is precisely how negative affirmations work), you will start to feel worthy.

As it turns out, self-worth is the foundation on which all personal growth is based. If I do not feel worthy, why invest time and energy in improving my life and the lives of people around me?

Words to Repeat

You might think that the words you need to repeat are magical. They are not. Instead, they are something we might say to others but rarely say to ourselves.

I like myself.
I love myself.

Speak them out loud. Say them with passion. Look yourself in the eye. Use every opportunity, from the bathroom mirror to a traffic stop. The more often you'll say them with conviction, the stronger the neural pathways in your brain will become. Those were the instruction that Brian Tracy gave.

When I tried to utter the words in front of a mirror, I felt as silly as I'd ever felt. I could not finish the sentences on my first attempt and had to look away. I kept trying. The murmurs grew, and the eye contact became steady.

Yet, I was unaware of the amount of negative self-talk this experiment would set off. Parts of my mind rebelled and spewed poison, everything from labeling myself as conceited and self-centered to calling the effort laughable. Nonetheless, I pressed on.

Getting to Neutral

It took several weeks for me to get to neutral. When I could finally say, *"I like myself, I love myself,"* without silly shivers or snide internal remarks, I felt like a remarkable milestone had been reached. Getting to neutral felt better than I had hoped. So, I kept going.

The Outcome

Because of the continued use of these affirmations, I no longer question my worth. Today, I can easily say the words "I like myself, I love myself," and just like when I tell my kids and my wife that I love them, there is no hesitation or reservation.

In hindsight, increasing self-worth was the foundation that allowed me to get sober, start a family, write thirty books, and go after my goals and dreams. Honestly, I am still my worst critic, but I only criticize my actions—which I can change—never who I am.

Try It For Yourself

I urge you to try these words for yourself. Even if you have to struggle as I did—no, especially if you have to struggle—push through. Shake off silliness and silence the inner critic by creating new neural pathways through repetition and conviction.

I like myself.
I love myself.

They might become the most important words you ever say to yourself.

Should Have to Next Time

Here's a common refrain when things don't go as planned: "I should have done this. I should have done that. I should've, I should've, I should've…." What follows is usually an internal emotional bashing that can be avoided. As Tony Robbins said so elegantly, *"people should all over themselves."*

What Does "Should Have" Mean?

Since we all do it, few people stop to think about what they are saying when they employ this habit of speech. Yet, the words spell out the meaning. "Should have" means that we want to change the past.

That begs the question: How does the brain respond when we wish for the impossible? When you say that you "should have," no course of action is available. You can't do anything about the past. So, the brain looks for alternate actions. Often, the only option left is to blame and shame.

Emotional Bashing

"What was I thinking? I'm so stupid. I should have prepared better. I should have said something else. I should have kept my mouth shut."

Because the focus is on the past, this spiraling thought process only leads to more blaming and shaming. I've met with clients weeks and months after they made a mistake and found that they were still stuck in an endless loop of self-blame.

Shifting the Focus

There is a better way. Instead of focusing on something entirely out of your control—the past—you can shift focus to what you can control—the present (and, by extension, your future, at least the thoughts, words and deeds you can control).

The Magic of "Next Time"

Shifting the focus to the future is empowering. Instead of creating a blame infinity loop, you can say, "next time." The magic is that your attention immediately shifts to the future. Your brain starts thinking about solutions for what you can do better. Once you have something to do, something to focus on that can make a difference, feelings of shame diminish. You'll have to revisit the past for them to resurface.

Next Time Examples

To cement this idea, let me give you a few examples.

- Next time, I'll be better prepared.
- Next time, I'll think things through.
- Next time, I'll pause before I speak.
- Next time, I'll ask for more time.
- Next time, I'll pay more attention.
- Next time, I'll say "next time" instead of "should have."

Notice that the key ingredient is what you can control. Focus on what you can do next time rather than expecting others to act differently. That way, you'll have more success.

Shifting is Hard

Look. I'm not gonna lie to you. As simple as this sounds, the actual implementation is difficult. You will need to set an intention to focus on the future and ensure that this intention is top of mind. It'll take mindfulness. And effort. And when the mind wanders—as it does naturally—and you forget, you'll need to remind yourself that it is okay to make mistakes. Having a sense of humor helps.

The Futility of "Should Have"

Whether or not you shift from "should have" to "next time," take a moment right now to recognize the futility of "should have." You cannot change the past. Let me repeat. You cannot change the past. If you continue to engage in such wishful thinking, it will only lead to more emotional pain. Therefore, choose another tactic if "next time" is not palatable.

Models

"There is only one corner of the universe you can be certain of improving, and that's your own self."

Aldous Huxley

Self-Directed Learning

The Boyatzis model of self-directed learning, created by American psychology expert Richard E. Boyatzis, is one of my favorite frameworks when working with clients. It's straightforward and effective.

Here is my interpretation of the five-step model.

1. Ideal Self

The first step revolves around imagining your ideal self, the dream version of you, including the character, skills, and attitudes you want to mold.

2. Real Self

The second step commands complete honesty because it is impossible to bridge the gap between the ideal and real selves if the starting point is an illusion. Most people tend to judge themselves either as better or as worse than they are. Therefore, it's wise to get help. With honest mirroring, your answers will likely be closer to the truth.

3. Learning and Action Agenda

The third step involves the construction of a realistic learning and action plan to bridge the gap between the ideal self and the real self. Once you know what you need to learn and what actions you want to take, you can move to the fourth step.

4. Experimentation

The fourth step involves experimentation with new thoughts and actions, building new neural pathways through repetition. Experimentation involves a certain amount of failure. It is to be expected. Experimentation also requires flexibility and the willingness to change the approach if something is not working.

5. Resonant Relationships

The fifth step is about forming trusting relationships with people that have similar goals or people who have made similar changes as the ones you are aiming for. In the fifth step, it is imperative to choose coaches, role models, and friends that will support you on your path.

What Is So Great About This Model?

One thing that sets the Boyatzis model apart from other models is the focus on the gap between the ideal self and the real self. Just like looking at a map, you can only go where you want to go once you know where you are.

Another unique thing is the circular relationship between steps (3) learning and action agenda, (4) experimentation, and (5) resonant relationships. Each affects the other. You create a plan, experiment, get feedback, tweak the agenda… and on it goes until you reach your desired outcome. This interaction allows for continuous course correction.

Example of the Five Steps

1. Suppose the dream for my ideal self is to become more loving and forgiving.
2. Through honest reflection, I realize that my real self has become irritable and

short-fused due to sustained external difficulties.

3. My learning and action agenda would consist of reading books about love and forgiveness, making a list of people I need to forgive, learning about the gap between external stimulation and my reactions, and creating affirmations for my desired behavior.

4. My experimentation could include loving-kindness meditation, taking longer to respond to people and circumstances (trying to avoid knee-jerk reactions), periods of deep breathing, and asking for forgiveness when I overstep boundaries.

5. The resonant relationship might be with a friend, a coach, or a spiritual advisor; any person who can support me and mirror how I am progressing.

In this example, progress would never look like a straight line from A to B. Once I'd start experimenting, feedback from my actions would guide me. I might need to go back and readjust my learning and action agenda, utilize my relationships to make sense of the outcomes, or even go back to step one and create a new vision of my ideal self based on the realities I have encountered.

The Mind is a Computer

I created this metaphor in the late 90s and have used it in my lectures, workshops, and coaching sessions ever since. It's pretty simple. If the mind is like a computer, these are the components:

Keyboard = Attention
Screen = Awareness
Hard Drive = Subconscious mind
Internet = Super-Conscious mind
Hardware = Body

Let's take a closer look at each component.

Keyboard = Attention

The keyboard is the gatekeeper. To get onto a computer's hard drive, it must first pass through the keyboard. Even though programs may get downloaded onto the hard drive, they almost always originate on someone's keyboard.

The same is true with the mind. Nothing gets in unless you give it attention. Attention is the keyboard. It is the basis for all intake of information, the starting point for all changes in the mind.

Screen = Awareness

Mental awareness is restricted in the same way a computer screen can only show a small portion of everything in a computer system. People are only aware of a fraction of their attitudes, thoughts, emotions, and knowledge.

Hard Drive = Subconscious Mind

The subconscious mind has many things in common with the computer hard drive. Every new computer includes free software that has already been installed. The same is true of humans. Any parent who has interacted with their child from birth knows that a child shows distinct characteristics and tendencies at a very early age. Whether we think that is related to genetics, astrology or karma, no parent can deny that the human personality starts forming at birth or sooner. Still, just like computer owners use free software disproportionately, humans also seem to be able to choose which personality traits get more or less attention and nurturing.

During the first years of life, other people directly influence the programming of a child's mind. The child walks around with the keyboard facing away, looking for guidance from its surroundings. The programs installed during this time differ substantially. Some are no good at all, which explains why some adults spend much of their life trying to reprogram attitudes and beliefs they adopted in childhood. Many people exert considerable energy trying to change their ideas, thoughts, beliefs and attitudes without getting results, mainly because they don't know a programming language that can help them get better results.

This would be the perfect time to introduce a programming language for the human mind, a method that works perfectly every time and changes attitudes and beliefs instantly. Unfortunately, and despite many proclamations to the contrary, that kind of programming language does not exist yet. However, *three things* can aid your reprogramming efforts.

Repetition – The more often you think, say or do something, the more likely you are to change your underlying attitude or belief in accordance with your repeated thoughts, words or actions.

Intense emotion – When strong emotions are linked to a thought process, actions, or experiences, fewer repetitions are needed to influence the underlying attitude. Unfortunately, this refers to both negative and positive emotions.

First-person perspective – Thinking and talking in the first person substantially influences the programming of a new attitude or belief in the subconscious mind.

If you use these three together, the results can be quite effective. You can generate new beliefs and attitudes by thinking and talking more often about what you want with strong positive emotions in the first person singular.

To minimize the power of destructive or debilitating attitudes, don't repeat thoughts, words, or actions related to that attitude as often. You can even try speaking about the old attitude in the third person, such as "the old program." Example: "I am compassionate and self-confident. The old program was negative and awkward."

It seems simple, but these three elements are everywhere when you start looking.

For instance, long-term memory is based on repetition, intense emotions and a first-person perspective. You are likelier to remember things from your childhood that occurred often and something that had a strong emotional effect on you, whether good or bad. On the other hand, you are less likely to remember the things that happened rarely or sporadically unless they had a strong emotional effect or you took them personally.

Advertising agencies and social media companies obviously know this language and try to present merchandise and services to the public with constant repetition, strong emotions, and personal appeal.

Learning from them, you could start forming your own internal marketing campaigns using first-person messaging (I), strong emotions, and constant repetition.

Internet = Super-Conscious Mind

The Internet could easily be the most exciting part of the computer metaphor. In short, it pertains to the part of the mind that philosophers, psychologists, and other scholars have named the super-conscious, collective unconscious, or over-mind. Many conflicting ideas have been set forth about the purpose, origin and possibilities of this part of the mind. Still, most players in this field agree that deep reflection, meditation, relaxation, and a variety of other practices allow people to access and activate this part of the mind. Unfortunately, we don't have enough factual information to make a strong case for how to use it effectively. I continue to follow that research and encourage you to do the same.

Hardware = Body

In the same way that computer hardware determines what software can be used, the human body influences control over the mind. Pain, constricted mobility, illnesses, and addictions can limit mental abilities. It's easier to control the mind when the body is reasonably healthy. That being said, it's important to remember that many physically disabled people have gained better control over their minds than the rest of us.

What Can You Control?

A computer owner can only control the *keyboard*—including the mouse and touchscreen. Only through the keyboard can the owner influence what happens on the screen and activate or deactivate programs on the hard drive.

In the same way, the only thing that you can learn to control is your *attention*. If you want to influence or change programs embedded in the subconscious mind, you must first improve your ability to focus.

Other Ways to Interpret the Model

There are various other ways to interpret the idea that the mind is like a computer.

From a mindfulness perspective, you can tidy up and declutter your screen.

From a Jungian shadow-self perspective, there are programs hidden on the drive that sometimes activate and cause havoc.

Knowing where those programs are and how to respond would be helpful.

From a physical perspective, we need to take better care of the hardware.

The computer comparison is most relevant because computers are modeled after the human mind and are meant to be a simplified version of the brain's processing power.

Stages of Learning

The four stages of learning have been attributed to Gordon Training International employee Noel Burch, although some attribute this model to Abraham Maslow. Even though most people know this model by now, it's worth revisiting it from time to time. The following is a simplified explanation.

1. I Don't Know That I Don't Know

The first stage is *unconscious incompetence*. You do not understand or know how to do something, do not necessarily recognize the deficit, and may even deny the skill's usefulness. To overcome this first stage, you must recognize the incompetence and see value in learning something new.

2. I Know That I Don't Know

The second stage is *conscious incompetence*. At this stage, you do not understand or know how to do something but recognize the deficit and value of making improvements.

3. I Know That I Know

The third stage is *conscious competence*. This is the stage of intentional and continuous practice and focus. You must focus intently so as not to forget.

4. I Don't Know That I Know

The fourth stage is *unconscious competence*. Skills are displayed without any effort. The thought or behavior has become part of your character, often described as second nature.

Driving Example

At some point, you did not know that driving was something you did not know how to do (stage 1). A desire to learn was born when you realized that you did not know how to drive (stage 2). In the early stages of driving, you needed to focus intently on every move, careful not to make mistakes (stage 3). After driving for several years, you hardly have to think about driving (stage 4).

Why Is This Important?

When we were children, it was socially acceptable to admit that we didn't know something or even to acknowledge that we didn't know what we didn't know.

However, as we aged, not knowing became embarrassing, especially when it was something that other people did easily and well.

By accepting these stages of learning, we take the pressure off. It's okay to realize, "Hey, I don't know how to do this."

And if we decide to do something about it—because, let's face it, we don't need to know how to do everything—it's also okay to have to focus, practice and fail while attaining the skill or ability. It's just a part of the learning process.

The Seven Energies

Energy is a lot like electricity. We cannot see electricity and do not understand its origin well, but we use it all the time. Likewise, people use the term energy all the time to describe their physical, emotional and mental states. They are either full of energy, don't have enough energy, or are running low on energy, and they talk about other people having or not having energy all the time. This way of relating to energy is not mystical, farfetched or imaginary but entirely natural and embedded in our language and culture.

Ancient yogic inquiries uncovered an elaborate material, emotional, mental and spiritual energy system. The philosophy of the seven energy centers or chakras (energy wheels) was the basis of my 2006 book, *The Seven Human Needs*. In that book, I attempted to explain the energy centers in a practical and metaphorical context and simultaneously relate them to modern motivational and psychological material emphasizing practical application.

The seven energy centers are a wellspring of information and inspiration that a short chapter will not suffice to explain everything I have learned and derived from that philosophy. Still, here are some of the core ideas.

Please note that the following overview is an interpretation of what the energy centers stand for, where they are situated in relation to the body and what elements and human needs they represent.

1. Survival and Material Energy (Earth) - situated at the base of the spine and represents the need for security.

2. Sensory, Creative, Sexual and Pleasure Energy (Water) - situated near the reproductive organs and represents the need for excitement and creativity.

3. Power and Self-Worth Energy (Fire) - situated slightly above the navel (solar plexus) and represents the need for individual strength.

4. Emotional Energy (Air) - situated near the heart and represents the need for love and relationships.

5. Expressive, Relational and Awareness Energy (Ether) - situated in the throat area and represents the need for expression and contribution.

6. Intellectual, Intuitive, Purpose and Being Energy (Consciousness) - situated in the forehead between the eyes and represents the need for wisdom and growth.

7. Spiritual, Non-dual and Existential Energy (Supreme Consciousness) - situated slightly above the top of the head and represents nonduality and the need for spirituality.

When connected to the body-mind-soul diagram, the first energy center represents the body, the second to the sixth centers represent the mind and emotions, and the seventh center represents the Self or soul.

The first thing people often notice when they look at a map of the human energy system is how complex a human being is. Different energies and needs can pull a person in various directions. That is why it's important to find a balance between these energies or needs so that we can focus on our priorities.

Energy Center Questionnaire

I created the following questionnaire as an indicator of energy imbalances. It's a tool for reflection more than a tool for diagnosis. A yes answer will mean that you are fairly balanced—I use the word fairly because I've found that perfect balance is rare—while a no answer will mean the opposite. If you create a scale from 1 to 10 between yes and no and place your answers on that scale, you may find the questionnaire more accurate.

1. Survival, Security and Material Energy

- Do you have enough money and material security?
- Do you have an adequate housing arrangement?
- Do you have a secure job or stream of income?
- Do you earn more than you spend?
- Do you feel safe and secure?
- Do you take good care of your health?

2. Sensory, Sexual and Pleasure Energy

- Do you feel excited and passionate about life?
- Are you directing and constructively releasing your sexual energy?
- Are you in control of your senses most of the time?
- Have you found an adequate balance between pleasure and discipline?
- Are you free from addiction?

3. Power, Self-Worth and Strength Energy

- Are you an energetic individual?
- Are you happy with your levels of self-worth and self-confidence?
- Do you like yourself?
- Can you use your personal power without repressing other people or making them feel inferior?

4. Emotional Energy

- Are your emotions balanced?
- Do you easily express love and affection?
- Do you easily forgive yourself and others?
- Do you take full responsibility for your emotions?

- Do you attempt to put yourself in other people's shoes to understand them better?
- Do you laugh often and easily?

5. Expressive and Relational Energy

- Can you express your thoughts and emotions easily?
- Do you communicate clearly and effectively?
- Are you an honest person?
- Do you share your knowledge and wisdom with others?
- Is there consistency between what you say and what you do?

6. Intellectual and Intuitive Energy

- Do you crave more wisdom and knowledge?
- Do you study regularly in your field of interest and expertise?
- Do you rely on your intuition as well as your intelligence?
- Does your life have a purpose?
- Do you contemplate the mysteries of life?

7. Spiritual and Non-dual Energy

- Do you meditate, pray, or contemplate regularly?
- Are you drawn to spiritual teachings?
- Have you experienced peace of mind, enlightenment, or a mystical union?

Reflect on your answers to these questions, and feel free to make your list of questions related to each center. If you find an imbalance, get to work. With continued awareness, you should experience more balance in your life.

The Mind is Fertile Soil

This model is an interpretation of a metaphor by Earl Nightingale in an audio lecture titled *The Strangest Secret*, where he compared the mind to fertile soil and thoughts to seeds. The most important principle to consider is that fertile soil is neutral. It doesn't matter whether you sow weeds, flowers or edibles; all will flourish in neutral soil. To further entertain the metaphor, here are four laws of nature that can be applied to the human mind.

Law 1) It Takes Time

If you start sowing today, you will not reap a good harvest tomorrow. People often become impatient when they start a new regimen of self-improvement and expect immediate results, but change takes time.

- This law teaches patience.

Law 2) Accept the Results

Time passes from planting to harvest. Your current mindset reflects the last time you sowed seeds. You must accept the results of what you were doing before you can reap something new.

- This law teaches acceptance.

Law 3) Weeds Grow

If you've ever tried cultivating a garden, you know two things. One, it's hard work to grow the plants you want. Two, you don't have to nurture weeds; they grow without help. Sadly, the same goes for negativity, irritation and other destructive attitudes and emotions.

- This law teaches us to beware of the weeds in our minds.

Law 4) Growing or Withering

Stagnation is not a natural state. In nature, things are either growing or withering, flourishing or dying. The same holds true for individuals.

- This law reminds us to keep growing.

The Implications

If your mind is neutral soil, contemplate the implications of this metaphor. To grow something new, you have to sow something new. You have to nurture and weed. Getting a new harvest takes time. Oh, and doing nothing does not mean things will stay the same. Keep growing.

Creating New Habits

The Greatest Salesman in the World by Og Mandino is an excellent book about habits and character building. Mandino tells readers that habits already control them and are masters of their actions, whether conscious or unconscious. Naturally, he suggests the formation of new and better habits. Mandino says that marinating the mind is the only way to embrace and incorporate a habit. Each habit is outlined in a short chapter, and readers are encouraged to read the book in a specific manner, focusing on one chapter each month, reading it three times a day for those thirty days, upon waking, in the middle of the day and before retiring for the night.

Another book, arguably best known for its emphasis on habit formation, is *The Seven Habits of Highly Effective People* by Steven Covey. Covey's philosophy is also based on the idea of character building. He rejects quick fixes without any effort.

I highly recommend both of these books.

The greatest thing about habits is that they equal autopilot. Take brushing your teeth, for example. Once that becomes a habit, you don't have to constantly chant positive affirmations or remind yourself to brush your teeth. It's simply a habitual part of what you do every day.

The Key is to Practice

Imagine:

- a concert pianist who practices for eight to ten hours a day.
- a Shaolin monk who repeats a forty-second routine for over four hours every day until the moves become a part of his automatic nervous reflexes.
- a basketball player that stays after practice and continues until she has hit twenty penalty shots and ten three-pointers in a row.
- a nun who meditates for hours upon hours every day and practices compassion towards her fellow humans, although they rarely reciprocate.

- a five-year-old kid who stays outside trying to ride his bike for as long as it takes for him to succeed.

Twenty-One Days?

Does it only take twenty-one days to develop a habit? It depends. Sometimes it takes a shorter time, sometimes longer, and sometimes old habits are so hard to break that new ones never take hold. The twenty-one-day idea is popular because it points people toward repetition and gives them an achievable deadline to work toward.

Four Steps

No matter the timeframe, if you want to incorporate a new habit, you need to take the following four steps:

1. Find Compelling Reasons: Write down why you want to incorporate the new habit and be clear. The reasons should move you to action.

2. Repeat Your Thoughts and Behavior: Repetition is the mother of skill. Repeat whatever it is you want until it sticks with you.

3. Persevere: Keep going when you don't feel like doing what you set out to do. Self-discipline has been defined as *"doing what you say you are gonna do, when you say you are gonna do it, as well as you can, whether you feel like it or not."*

4. Maintain: Once established, create a plan to maintain the habit.

The Two Phases

During the creation of a habit, you need to put in time and effort. The beginning stages can take anywhere from a few hours to a few years to a lifetime. Effort and energy expenditure differs. The development stage requires time, concentration and sacrifices. In the beginning, make sure you have a good plan because you don't want to waste time on practices that do not produce results or go against your priorities in life.

Maintenance doesn't take nearly as much energy or time as the developmental stage. To maintain a habit, follow a simple rule: *Use it or lose it!* It's a shame to see how many people have put a lot of time and effort into gaining something only to lose it from lack of use.

Balance Development and Maintenance

The traps here are simple. You can, for example, stay in the developmental stage too long, putting too much time and effort after you have mastered something, which is an unwise use of resources. Or you can start maintenance too early before fully cementing the habit, thereby restarting the developmental phase.

Brian Tracy said, "*bad habits are easy to form but hard to break; good habits are hard to form but easy to live with.*"

Keep that in mind.

Six Steps of Learning

The following six steps of learning are immensely helpful, both when situating yourself in a learning situation and when guiding others. At first glance, they appear deceptively simple, but if you take the time to contemplate their implications, they will serve you in all learning situations.

1. Learn
2. Digest and Evaluate
3. Use
4. Benefit and Re-evaluate
5. Teach
6. Serve

Step 1) Be a Willing Student

Learning requires humility and receptiveness. Many people hear the same lecture or read the same book, but only those open to learning will benefit. As the saying *"when the student is ready, the teacher appears"* implies, learning depends not only on the teacher's ability to teach but also on the student's willingness to learn.

Step 2) Extract the Essence

Just like food needs digestion to extract nutrients, information must be digested for value. Once accumulated, it's important to compare what you've learned to what you already know. Further digestion could include imagining what life would look like if you applied what you've learned. This helps you decide whether to move ahead.

Step 3) Take Action

Use what you've learned. Only then will it start to improve your life.

Step 4) Take Inventory

Is your life better after taking action? Have you benefitted? Were the promises upheld? If the answers to these questions are yes, great. Continue. If the answers are no, think about why. Was the information faulty? Do you need to go back to step one and review it? More often than not, one or two revisions of the material are required, even if you are getting benefits.

Step 5) Look at New Perspectives

Why is teaching a part of the learning process? Because you need to look at the information from a variety of different perspectives to be able to teach it. Instead of limiting yourself to your perspective, you'll have to put yourself in other people's shoes and think about how you can best present the information to them. Teaching will deepen your understanding.

Step 6) Give

Once you've embodied the information by using it in your own life and examined it from many perspectives by teaching it to others, it is fair to say that you've graduated. But the final step in this process reminds you to pay it forward by serving others. Whether through continued teaching, mentoring, or altruistic actions is up to you.

The Hardest Step

In this model, the most challenging step is taking action. Most people only put a fraction of what they already know into action. In fact, two of my favorite coaching and training questions are (a) how much of what you already know have you put to use? and (b) how would your life improve if you used more of what you already know?

Don't Be a Parrot

Sadly, too many people jump straight from the first step to the fifth. They start teaching without experience by parroting (repeating) information they've just been fed. Some say that those who can't do, teach. Turn that on its head. Before you teach, do.

Not in Textbooks

I've used this model in my lectures and books for over twenty years, but it did not come from a textbook. Rather, it came from an inscription by my mentor and friend, Yogi Shanti Desai. I've studied many learning models since and have yet to come across one as simple, elegant, and useful as his.

Seeking Help

"Our prime purpose in this life is to help others. And if you can't help them, at least don't hurt them."

Dalai Lama

Why People Seek Help

I've found that people seek help for two primary reasons.

- They've experienced *pain* and want to reduce it.
- They've made *improvements* and want more.

I know this is an oversimplification. Still, I've found that people's reasons generally fall into one of these categories, and I've been teaching, training, and coaching for over twenty years.

The people who don't seek help are somewhere in between. Their lives are not bad enough to want something better and not good enough to want more. Henry David Thoreau described them as leading *"lives of quiet desperation."* The in-betweeners probably need help but don't seek it.

Pain Depends on Intensity

Think of physical pain. If you have a few mosquito bites, you will try to suffer through the discomfort, but if your leg is broken, you'll scream for immediate help. In the same way, your need for help from a friend, personal coach, counselor, therapist, workshop, or religious leader will depend on the intensity of your pain.

Improvements Depend on Desire

Let's say you get a grade of 90 in math. Do you get a tutor and push yourself closer to a 100, or are you satisfied with a 90? That depends on your desire for betterment. In this context, it's interesting that most overachievers have coaches. They feel a strong desire to keep improving, even when they are good at something.

Personal Examples

It's easy to talk about "people in general," so let me give you personal examples.

I made a mess of my life before I first sought help. In my early twenties, I dropped out of college, struggled with alcohol abuse, smoked two to three packs a day, could not create long-term relationships, and my finances were a mess. My situation kept getting worse until, one day; I'd had enough. I sought help from the twelve-step community, therapists, friends, spiritual teachers, and motivational speakers and read books about all of my ailments—lots of books. It worked. I found sobriety and turned my life around.

That started a building phase in my life. I married, started a business, had kids, bought my first apartment, and made more money in one year than I'd made in the previous two or three years. I wanted more. Again, I sought help from coaches, financial advisors, business leaders, more books, therapists, and anyone else who would advise me.

Polarities Push Buttons

I've studied human behavior most of my life —first to understand my own, then to help others—and I can't explain exactly why people seek help because of these polarities. It's probably tied to a boatload of underlying factors, from human needs to emotional constitutions. All I know is that if someone seeks my help, it is usually because they are experiencing pain or have started attaining some success.

Vulnerability and Pain

When people feel pain, they want to get rid of it as quickly as possible. It's human nature. Nothing wrong with that. However, there are several industries centered on pain relief, and many use immoral ways to take advantage of people when they are weak, thusly increasing pain rather than reducing it. Here, I will focus on the coaching profession and promises to relieve emotional and mental pain. Some of the warnings can be applied to other industries as well.

Snake Oil in Coaching

According to Wikipedia: *"Snake oil is a term used to describe deceptive marketing, health care fraud, or a scam. Similarly, "snake oil salesman" is a common expression used to describe someone who sells, promotes, or is a general proponent of some valueless or fraudulent cure, remedy, or solution. [1] The term comes from the "snake oil" that used to be sold as a cure-all elixir for many kinds of physiological problems."*

In the coaching marketplace, signs of 'snake oil' are relatively similar. Look for unrealistic promises, quick fixes, total transformation, and psychological altering.

1. Unrealistic Promises

When something sounds too good to be true, it usually is. When you feel good and stable, you'll have a reliable BS meter to guide you, but when you are in pain, vulnerability often disables that meter. Your need for immediate relief can blind you.

I consider myself savvy, but it took me over a decade to learn this, and the price was high financially and emotionally. To guard against unrealistic promises, read or listen to Martin Seligman's book, *What You Can Change and What You Can't*. In addition to your BS meter, it will help you see the difference between realistic and unrealistic promises.

2. Quick Fixes

Change takes time. There is no way around that. I've seen too many coaches offer quick fixes and then keep charging people session after session, year after year, because the change hasn't quite stuck. "We just have to go a little deeper. We'll get it this time," is the promise that keeps going unfulfilled. The quick-fix deception also overlooks a crucial psychological fact: Change does not come from the outside. Other people cannot change you. They can guide and assist you, but you do all the work. You make changes. I've seen quicker-than-usual improvements in my coaching practice, but they build upon what people already know and tap into their existing motivations.

3. Total Transformation

I used to be a believer in total transformation. Over time, I've come to see that there is something inherently wrong with the concept. Those who believe they need to replace everything and start from scratch are operating in the false belief that they have nothing good to build on. I can go along with the idea of evolution—such as a change from a caterpillar to a butterfly—but some people promise that you can transform from a caterpillar to a tiger.

To repeat, all improvements start where people already are. They can only improve and evolve from there. Furthermore, it's impossible to tear everything down and start from zero. Still, in a state of pain and weakness, total transformation can sound appealing. Wouldn't it be great if we could just start over? But that's not reality. We can improve, definitely, but promises of total transformation are empty and usually lead to more pain.

4. Psychological Altering

Some coaches may act like it, but we are not trained psychologists. I recently did a podcast interview with Dr. Robyn Odegaard, a psychologist, and she told me that too many coaches are dabbling in her field without proper training. When a coach offers to change your beliefs, reduce your pain, work on your family history (Dr. Odegaard said that was a big no, no because family stuff is complicated), or cure you from addiction, to name a few common non-coaching promises, you may want to look somewhere else for help. Again, in a state of pain, all of these promises sound enticing, but they are neither realistic nor are coaches the right people to work with on psychological issues.

Great Coaches Out There

I hope I haven't scared you with these warnings. There are great coaches out there, people with integrity who work with their clients to produce outstanding results, everything from clarity and increased productivity to mindfulness and fuller spiritual lives. Just be aware that your judgment may be somewhat clouded when you are in pain.

Final Thing to Watch Out For

That brings me to my final thing to watch out for: Pressure sales techniques.

The coaching market is crowded, so some people have started using manipulative sales methods to strong-arm vulnerable people into buying.

This is highly unethical.

You must enter into a coaching relationship willingly because it depends on cooperation. When you have a discovery call with a coach, make sure you have time to think about your options and aren't sucked into a long-term program with over-the-top promises and short-term bargains. Sleep on it overnight before you make big decisions. At the very least, start by scheduling fewer than four sessions to see if the coach is right for you.

Get Appropriate Help

If you are in pain and looking for solutions, try to use a measure of discernment. I've seen well-educated people lose their ability to think logically and try outlandish things because they or their loved ones were in pain. Keep looking and trust that the appropriate help is out there for you.

Working With a Coach

Lots of people have stereotypes in mind when it comes to personal coaching. "It's just a bunch of people at Starbucks giving sketchy advice about how to live, right?" Not quite. The profession has evolved over the past twenty years. Coaches vary from person to person, but here are some things you can expect when working with a personal coach.

1. Focus on an Outcome

The relationship begins with the end in mind. A seasoned coach will know how to ask questions that will assist you in crafting worthy ideals and goals.

2. Motivation

Motivation is like an internal undercurrent that pulls you in the right direction, even if you try to swim against it. Because of its inner nature, no one can create motivation for you, but a coach can help you find motivating reasons and anchor them to your goals.

3. Strategies

Imagine sitting down with someone and looking at a map. After you point to where you want to go, the other person will ask, "How do you plan to get there?" Together, you look at possible paths, discuss modes of transportation, and talk about what to do if you run into obstacles or feel like giving up. Based on that discussion, you can decide on a strategy that works for you. The same is true for your goals. A coach can help you choose the best path and methods to reach your desired destination.

4. Support

No matter your journey, obstacles are inevitable. A personal coach can support you as you explore solutions, overcome limiting beliefs, and build self-confidence.

5. Self-Reliance

What separates professional coaches from those who want to keep you in an ongoing, never-ending, costly relationship is a focus on self-reliance. Everyone needs help from time to time. That's why coaches exist. But the end goal has to be self-reliance. In a healthy coaching relationship, you'll start to trust yourself more and rely on the coach less.

Setting Expectations

Hopefully, these ideas will help you set expectations when entering a coaching relationship. At a minimum, look for someone who can help you work toward a clear outcome, offers strategies and support, and believes in self-reliance. That said, too many expectations can get in the way. Once you've done your due diligence, trust the process and be open to possibilities.

Mindfulness Coaching

Mindfulness is a state of calm and conscious presence. It can help you improve sleep, deal with stress, be more creative, regulate emotions, and increase focus... to name a few. There are four main areas where a mindfulness coach can help you.

1. Evaluation

A coach can help you evaluate your life to see where you feel most stressed or least present and help you determine how you could benefit from mindfulness.

2. Choosing Practices

The variety of mindfulness practices is immense and includes everything from physical awareness to nature walks, breathing techniques, mindful eating, contemplative prayer, meditation, and much more. You can't possibly practice all of them. Helping you find practices that fit your life and character is at the heart of what a mindfulness coach does.

3. Creating Habits

Once you've chosen practices, a mindfulness coach can work with you to make them habitual. Once a habit, mindfulness becomes an effortless part of your life.

4. Setting Intention Goals

To bring mindfulness into more areas of life, a coach can also help you set intention goals. They differ from 'outcome' or 'habit' goals in one way; the intention remains the same, but the methods can change.

What To Look For

In essence, you are looking for competency, empathy and some knowledge of your situation. People listen to people who are like them.

I, for one, have taught meditation, breathing, and relaxation since 1997. I've also been in fast-paced business environments, spent years being the primary caretaker for my kids while my wife traveled for work, and dealt with various difficulties, from alcohol abuse and tinnitus to bankruptcy and losing a loved one. I can empathize with people in those situations.

If a soldier comes to me with PTSD, I usually refer them to veteran mindfulness teachers because they have greater empathy and knowledge of the problem.

Discovery Session

Book a discovery session with the coach you are considering. Talk about your situation, ask how they would work with you and inquire about their lives, including challenges and successes. If you find an acceptable blend of competency, empathy and knowledge, that's a great place to start.

About the Author

Gudjon Bergmann has authored thirty books, including two novels, two memoirs, a children's book, and nonfiction books on a variety of topics, such as goal setting, time management, stress, interfaith relations, yoga, spirituality, smoking cessation, nonfiction writing, meditation, and more.

Bergmann is an experienced Yoga Teacher, Ordained Interfaith Minister, Certified Life Coach, and Certified Mindfulness Teacher.

www.gudjonbergmann.com